God and I

God and I

A Book about Faith and Prayer
by
Iverna Tompkins
edited by Irene Burk Harrell

Logos International
Plainfield, New Jersey

Scripture is taken from the King James Version except where noted as RSV (Revised Standard Version), TAB (The Amplified Bible), TEV (Today's English Version) and TLB (The Living Bible). Parenthetical Scripture locations in the text do not necessarily mean that the immediately preceding words are quoted from any particular version of the Bible, but that a similar thought occurs in that location.

GOD AND I
Copyright © 1978 by Logos International
All rights reserved
Printed in the United States of America
International Standard Book Number: 0-88270-274-2
Library of Congress Catalog Card Number: 78-52396
Published by Logos International, Plainfield, N.J. 07060

To my brother Judson
whose example and encouragement
helped me discover
the privilege and power of prayer

Other books by Iverna Tompkins:

How to Be Happy in No Man's Land

How to Live with Kids and Enjoy It

Table of Contents

God and I

1

What Is Prayer?

"I used to pray a lot," a man told me one day. "But I have discovered it is not important for me to set aside a time of prayer. Instead, I just praise the Lord all the time."

I could hardly believe it, so I challenged him in order to make sure I had heard correctly.

"Are you telling me you no longer take a special time to spend alone with the Lord in petition and prayer?"

"That's right," he said. "I just praise the Lord as I go. I praise the Lord as I travel, I praise the Lord as I write books, I praise the Lord all the time. And I spend a good bit of time reading the Word to see if I have missed something."

He seemed to be satisfied with the results, but I could only see his attitude as one of limited obedience to God's Word:

Pray without ceasing. (1 Thess. 5:17)
Watch and pray. (Matt. 26:41)
In every thing by prayer and supplication . . . make your requests known unto God. (Phil. 4:6, KJV, NEB)
Continue in prayer. (Col. 4:2)
I will therefore that men pray everywhere. (1 Tim. 2:8)

1

But let him ask in faith. (James 1:6)
Praying always with all prayer and supplication.
(Eph. 6:18)
When ye pray. . . . (Matt. 6:7)

The Scriptures commanding us to pray are innumerable. God's people have always known that they ought to pray. But we seem to be extremists by nature, swinging wildly from one emphasis to another. As soon as a new teaching comes to the church, we act as if we've forgotten everything else we've ever learned, and we flock to the new ideas.

In my early years, the church did a lot of praying. We studied the importance of prayer and had "tarrying services" where the people prayed and prayed. Then, some years ago, the Lord began to teach His body that it needed to learn to praise and worship Him, speaking words of exaltation, praise, and love, raising up holy hands unto Him.

The new emphasis on praise and worship was exciting to me. It transformed my ministry as greatly as the Baptism in the Holy Spirit had changed it earlier. I thought I had reached Utopia, and that I could never learn anything more wonderful than this truth. I had thought that praising God meant saying, "Thank you, Lord." Then I learned there was a whole lot more to it than that. As I sang and spoke of His worthiness and greatness, praise paved the way to worship, and the benefits were unending.

If God's people had picked up praising God as the second wing of a prayer-and-praise-combination, we'd have made a lot of forward progress. But we didn't do anything as sensible as that. Instead, we clipped off the wing of prayer and put on the wing of praise. We were lopsided in one direction to begin with, and now we are lopsided in another direction.

One beautiful lesson Jesus taught is the lesson of balance which is the backbone of all good spiritual teaching.

We don't find this balance in the academic world. In order to teach mathematics effectively, the professor has to pretend it's the only subject, certainly the most important. In order for another professor to get his students to learn their English lessons, he may have to act as if the worlds of mathematics and science don't exist.

But as believers in Christ, we are called to mature until we are complete, lacking nothing. That means we can't let go of one good teaching just because we hear another one. We're to appropriate all that is of value and put each new teaching into proper perspective.

Today, the Lord is encouraging us to put the wing of prayer back where it belongs, keeping the wing of praise intact this time, bringing us to a greater degree of spiritual maturity than we've ever known before.

Praise is important, but praise doesn't eliminate the need for prayer.

I can remember trying to muster up a hunger for prayer in years gone by. Many times, when I was going through a dry spell, I tried to talk myself out of it by saying, "Iverna, you're really hungry for fellowship with God in prayer." But it didn't work. Sometimes, I even lied about it, crying out, "O Lord, as the hart panteth after the water brook, so cries my soul after thee, O God." But that didn't work either. The Holy Spirit didn't receive my lie. Instead, He said, "Your soul does not, Iverna. You're just trying to get through your hour." And I had to admit He was right.

But today things are different for me and for many more of God's people. The dryness is gone. One of the things God is restoring to the church is a true hunger for prayer.

Recently, in Spirit-filled groups, I have made it a point to ask the leaders if anything special was stirring among them. Without exception, they have replied something like this:

"Yes, something's going on all right, something exciting. A

renewal in prayer, you might call it. God's people are getting in touch with God and learning to enjoy His presence."

Christians everywhere are hearing a cry in their own spirits to pray as they've never prayed before. God has never played games with His people, and at last, they seem to be getting serious with Him.

We're in a day when a quick work of the Lord is taking place. The Father is revealing His Son through the corporate body of Christ. And we are learning that if we don't fulfill our responsibilities, we may not enjoy our privileges as members of that body.

The reason why many Christians are still not fulfilling their duty to pray is not that they are unwilling, but that they feel they don't know how to pray. Part of the problem is that they haven't understood what prayer is, nor why God tells His people to pray. We need to understand the true nature of prayer so that our prayers might become the effectual, fervent ones that God can use to produce His will among men on earth.

Prayer is not a process by which we give God information He doesn't already have. Prayer is not always presenting our "want list." Neither is it an end in itself; it is a means to an end. Our goal should not be just to pray but to receive the results of prayer—that indescribable fellowship with our beloved One in the holy place.

Suppose you decide to telephone me. You dial my number, but before the phone rings, you say, "Hello, Iverna. I just wanted to call you and talk to you a few minutes." You rattle on while the phone is ringing off the wall in my home, and finally you say, "Well, Iverna, it's sure been good talking to you. I'll be ringing you again one of these days." Then you hang up, and the phone stops ringing. When I come in later, I don't even know you've been on the line, because I was out at the time.

This is the way many people pray, making prayer an end instead of making it the means to fellowship with God. They never bother to pay any attention to whether or not God picks up the receiver to answer. Instead of really coming into His presence with thanksgiving and praise, they just give Him the list of things they want Him to do. Then they hang up before He has a chance to say hello.

It's possible for us to get up on Sunday morning, get dressed in our best, and go to God's house. While we're there, we sing His songs, read the letters He has written to us, talk about Him, maybe even talk to Him, and head for home. Then we meet someone on the way who asks, "Where have you been this morning?"

"I've been to the house of the Lord."

"Oh? Was He there?"

"I don't know. I was so busy doing things in His name, that I wasn't aware of His presence or absence."

When we are getting ready to spend some time with the Lord, we need first to establish a connection, entering His gates with thanksgiving, His courts with praise, and coming before His presence with singing (Ps. 100:2, 4).

"Lord, I thank you for this day. I thank you for all you have done for me, and I praise you for who you are. I praise you for your love." In the congregation, we worship Him in the Spirit, and sing before His presence to prepare ourselves to make our requests known to Him. When we have done these things, we have dialed His number, we've heard the phone ring, heard Him say hello on the other end of the line, and then we're ready to have a two-way conversation with Him.

Real prayer, meaningful conversation with God, is a dialogue, not a monologue. And it should follow the three basic rules of natural conversation.

First, in ordinary conversation, we are aware of the other person. God longs for our praise, our worship, our adoration. In Zephaniah, we read that He literally sings over us in joy (Zeph. 3:17). He attends our services of worship and joins our worshiping in praise to Him by singing His joy over us.

2. Second, in ordinary conversation, we take turns gracefully. There isn't anything less enjoyable than a conversation in which one person monopolizes the whole thing, no matter how interesting he might be. Everyone has a desire to contribute, and nobody is happy when one person usurps the entire discussion. We are expected to listen as well as to talk.

3. The third rule of ordinary conversation is that we talk about the thing the other person wants to talk about. We should not try to control the subject all the time ourselves. Most of us are professional subject changers, and this is never more evident than when we are on our knees talking to God.

I might begin my prayer time by saying, "Hello, Lord. I love you, I appreciate you, and I thank you for all the blessings you're putting into my life."

When I have come into His presence in that way, He might say, "Iverna, I'm glad you called today. I've been meaning to talk with you about something in your life."

Chances are, I already have more than a sneaking suspicion of what He wants to talk about. When God decides to talk to me about something, everything I read, everything I hear, every tape, every sermon, every ministry, every periodical I pick up, every Scripture that comes to my attention is talking about what He wants to talk about with me. I know there's no respite until I give up, but I usually keep resisting as long as I can.

"Please, Lord, I don't want to talk about that today. I've something else to tell you." I'll attempt to pray over the thing, under the thing, and around it in all directions, saying, "Let's talk about that later, Lord. Today I want to beseech you in behalf of my sister in the Lord—"

But God isn't interested in listening to that just now.

"Iverna!" (It's hard to ignore Him when He speaks to me in that tone of voice.) "Iverna, first let's deal with this thing in your life. Then we can talk about what *you* want."

If I don't give in and converse with Him on the subject He

has chosen, I have a very frustrating time of prayer. But if I put my own desires aside and talk about what He wants to talk about, He is able to make some progress in my life.

Dealing with the thing I want to avoid may take a minute; it may take an hour; it may take longer. But when it is dealt with, I am cleansed. Then, in His graciousness, the Lord says, "Now what was that you wanted to ask me to do, Iverna? Why was it you came to me this time?"

"Well, Lord, I wanted to come to you in behalf of so-and-so and ask you to bless her life. She's having such a struggle these days, and I'm believing you to move on her behalf."

He nods and says, "All right, Iverna. The effectual, fervent prayer of a righteous woman availeth much. I'll see what I can do for her."

In my traveling around the country, I meet a lot of interesting people. I have learned I can have really good fellowship with them if I talk about what they want to talk about.

I used to listen with only one thought in mind. If the other party mentioned God or church or religion or faith, I'd move in and take over in such an obnoxious way that the door of communication would be slammed between us. They'd back off in a hurry, thinking, "Oh-oh, another weirdo, another religious fanatic," and I'd lose them before I got started. But I've learned God can give us wisdom in these encounters and make us a blessing to people instead of a door slammer.

Sometimes when people ask me what I do for a living, I just say, "Well, I care for people." That usually intrigues them, and a really meaningful rapport might develop between us before the conversation is finished.

To me, the highest calling of a believer is to breathe in and breathe out. The Christ within us is able to do everything else that needs to be done. The Bible confirms this to me when it says that we are always to be ready to give an answer to any man that asks us the reason for the hope that is in us. If we go around trying to cram an answer down someone's throat when he hasn't asked a question, we're just being bores, not witnesses to the indwelling presence of the Lord Jesus Christ.

Before we go to our jobs in the morning we can say, "Lord, I'm going to my work this morning. Please let your presence go with me in such a way that my co-workers will see you in my actions and my attitudes. Let them see you in my very countenance, Lord." When we do that, amazing things can happen.

Once, while I was on vacation, a woman just walked up to me and said, "Excuse me, but I have a problem. Could you—"

I listened to her tale of woe, ministered the love of Jesus to her, and then asked, "Why did you choose me to talk to out of this great mob of people around here?"

"I don't know exactly," she admitted. "I was across the room when I first saw you, but somehow I knew instinctively that you could help."

She was just one person of many who have indicated to me that we don't have to run around with signboards hanging around our necks to let people know that Jesus is in our lives.

Prayer is the doorway to heaven, the key to fellowship with God. It is the hole in the sky that was revealed to Jacob, and God wants to commune with us in the same way, engaging in *two-way* conversation. Prayer is the vehicle that brings us into the holy place where we can receive from Him what He has caused us to desire in our hearts, for our good and His glory. In prayer, we open up a channel through which God can provide for us. Prayer gives Him a moral right to act in the situation we bring before Him.

Some people are turned off by the idea that we can learn to pray. Any time God tells me to speak on the subject of prayer, I expect a grand exodus. The enemy fights the subject of prayer more than any other, because prayer is such a powerful tool in the hands of believers. The world has been literally turned around by the power of prayer, and Satan knows it. Every great revival has been preceded by prayer.

One of the best ways to begin to pray is to bring the Word of God to Him and make it your own. You can simply say, "Yes, Lord," to the prayers that are written in His Word. You can appropriate the words and thoughts of the Scriptures for yourself and address them to God. We don't have to be original with Him. As a matter of fact, originality is impossible. The Bible tells us, "There is nothing new under the sun" (Eccles. 1:9, RSV).

We can also learn to pray by listening to the prayers of others. My secretary told me that for a whole year, her entire prayer life consisted of "Yes, Lord. Yes, Lord," because I was so loud in the prayer room. I'd be over in one corner on my knees, praying, "O God, I bring so-and-so to you . . ." and she'd be in another corner hearing me, adding her "amens" to what I was asking God to do. When God moved me away from her, she could pray on her own because she had listened so well. She'd learned to appropriate my prayers for herself. We all learn to pray by praying, not by reading books about prayer or listening to someone talk about the subject.

I had to learn to pray years ago when the Lord spoke to me one day and said, "I want you on your knees for one hour every morning."

Since I didn't know how to get out of the assignment, I asked the pastor to announce that there would be someone in the prayer room every morning from ten until eleven o'clock. The first day, one other person showed up. I went to one corner of the room, she went to the opposite corner, and we began to pray. I prayed for my family, my own life, every missionary I'd ever heard of, and then I prayed that God would save souls in our neighborhood. When I had finished all of that, I looked at my watch and saw that two and a half minutes had gone by.

"Lord, what will I do for the next fifty-seven and a half

minutes?" I cried. He didn't tell me, so I opened my Bible and read for a while, praying the parts of the Word that sounded like prayers, reading some more, praying some more, and after what seemed like forever, the time was gone. The next day, the hour didn't seem quite so interminable.

By the end of that year of having to stay on my knees for an hour every morning, I had learned to pray for four or five hours at a stretch without being aware of the passage of time.

If you haven't yet learned to pray, you might begin by setting a regular time to get on your knees and stay there for fifteen minutes or so. You could begin by saying, "Lord, for these few minutes, it is just the two of us. I want to hear what you're saying, and I want to make my needs known to you."

The first thing you know, what you began as a chore to be gotten through somehow, will have become the high point of your day.

The Scripture speaks of many ways of praying—crying out to God; pouring out your heart to Him and letting Him fill your heart; falling on your face before Him; praying with the understanding and with the Spirit. . . .

Praying with the Spirit is not always praying in an unknown tongue. Sometimes, the Holy Spirit makes supplication through us in words we *can* understand. No matter what the language, the Holy Spirit within us knows what to pray for each of us.

We don't need to categorize ourselves by saying, "I'm this kind of a pray-er or that kind of a pray-er." Because the Lord is Lord of our prayers, He is free to change our approach at any time. Sometimes He might whisper through us; sometimes He might shout. He may cry through us, exult through us, pray sentence prayers through us, or conduct us in a kind of conversational prayer.

Every kind of prayer can be beautiful. Silent prayer is fine when you're waiting in the doctor's office. Silent prayer would be foolish if you were asked to stand and lead a congregation in prayer.

To whom should we pray? In certain Scriptures—Matthew 6:6, John 16:23, Ephesians 1:17 and 3:14—we find directions for praying to God the Father. In other Scriptures, we find we can pray to the Son—Acts 7:59 and 2 Corinthians 12:8. We do not usually pray to the Holy Spirit, but He prays through us—John 14:16-17 and Romans 8:26.

When should we pray? "Pray without ceasing" (1 Thess. 5:17). That has to mean we should pray *all* the time. We find Scriptures indicating that Jesus prayed in the morning (Mark 1:35), in the evening (Matt. 14:23), all night (Luke 6:12), and in the daytime (Luke 9:18). That pretty well covers around-the-clock praying.

Some Christians are morning people. After nine o'clock at night, you have to poke them to keep them awake. Others are night owls. People are so different from one another, they naturally differ in their special times of prayer.

For me to set a time of prayer early in the morning is a tragedy. I can get my body out of bed early if I have to, but my mind doesn't usually join me until at least ten o'clock or so. And my voice may not get up until noon. Set a time that's right for you.

What is the proper posture for prayer? You may bow, you may kneel, you may stand, you may prostrate yourself on the floor, you may lie on your bed. Every one of these postures of prayer has scriptural backing.

Where can you pray? Wherever you are. You can pray in public or in private, in the desert, at church, at home, behind the wheel of your automobile at the traffic light, on the street corner, in your closet.

To me, entering into a closet to pray doesn't mean I have to crawl under the overcoats and sit among the smelly shoes to talk to God while I suffocate. It means I mentally enter into a closet and shut out all distractions. We can do that in the noisiest of prayer rooms if we put our minds to it.

Be yourself. Pray as you are led, wherever you are, whenever the need arises.

For what should we ask? We may ask for anything that is in line with His perfect will for us.

When Elijah asked Elisha what he wanted done for him before Elijah left, Elisha knew immediately what to ask for. The desire for a double portion of the spirit of Elijah was in his heart, and in asking for it, he received it.

Many Christians have gotten into the habit of just thanking the Lord, leaning on such Scriptures as, "Before they call, I will answer" (Isa. 65:24), and "Your Father knoweth what things ye have need of, before ye ask him" (Matt. 6:8). They have almost practiced *not* praying, not asking God for anything, and so they have forgotten how to pray. Their feeling seems to be, "If He knows everything already, and He supplies all our needs, why should we ask?" Only one answer is needed: "Because His Word tells us to ask."

2

How to Pray

Few people really feel comfortable with their own ability to pray. And yet the Bible teaches we are all capable of prayer. Each person who has received Christ into his life has been given the ability to enter His gates with thanksgiving, to enter His courts with praise, to come before His presence with singing (Ps. 100), and to walk boldly (Heb. 4:16) into the Holy of Holies, because the veil which separated God from the people was rent in twain (Matt. 27:51) when Christ was crucified. Every time we approach the Father in Jesus' name, the Father hears, "Jesus and I ask for thus and such a blessing." And because of His Son, He gives us the desire of our hearts (John 16:23).

We have a little better understanding of this when we realize we are being made sons of God. We have been adopted into His family, and the Spirit of the Lord witnesses in our hearts, crying, "Abba, Father" (Rom. 8:15). While we're doing this, the Son himself is making intercession for us (Heb. 7:25).

Still, even knowing these things, we have the feeling that we're not praying right, that we're not sufficiently eloquent, that *our* prayers lack power. We keep comparing our prayers with those of other people, and we have a tendency to imitate them in an effort to "improve" our own prayers.

We need to guard against this tendency. God doesn't want us to be pretending to be someone else when we come to Him in prayer. We're supposed to be ourselves, putting all imitation aside.

Jesus was no pretender. Something happened every time He prayed. And the results were so obvious in His life that the disciples longed to be able to pray as He prayed. Jesus didn't go to them and say, "Now, boys, it's time for you to learn to pray." The disciples came to Jesus and said, "Lord, teach us to pray" (Luke 11:1).

Jesus' prayers were effective. He knew who He was. He knew His position of authority with God. He knew the power was there. When He went to the grave of Lazarus, His prayer was preceded by His statement to God. In effect, He said, "God, I know you're in me. I know who I am. I understand your power, but so that all the people around me can know what's going to happen, I'm going to pray." Then He prayed aloud so the people could hear what He was saying to God.

When some people are called on to pray in a public gathering, they sound as if they're offering a prayer for the people around them to hear. When others pray, it's as if they don't know there are any people present. They're talking directly to God.

It is hard for us to agree with what is coming forth from the one who has been called on to pray if we sense a phoniness in the words. (They may sound more like tinkling cymbals and sounding brass than prayer to the eternal God.) It's wonderful when we sense that a person is *really* praying as he intones, "O matchless, gracious Father in heaven, thou who art omniscient and omnipotent, we beseech thee this day on behalf of thy people—" But it's tragic to teach that kind of prayer language to people who don't understand such words.

I was sitting on a platform one day, looking down on the people as they were "praising the Lord," and it seemed that the Lord said to me that some were really praising Him while others were merely reciting words of praise they had been taught.

"If you went to Africa and learned the native's language, would that make you a native?" He asked me.

"Of course not."

"Then what makes you think you've made natives out of all these just because you've taught them the language?"

I understood what He was getting at. It was a lesson I needed.

One of the hymns often sung as an invitational hymn begins, "Just as I am. . . ." We would do well to appropriate such a concept for our prayer lives, coming just as we are, without putting on airs or adopting a lofty vocabulary that is not comfortable in our mouths. Honesty and sincerity are prime requisites for our prayers. A woman in the New Testament learned that the hard way:

> Then Jesus went thence, and departed into the coasts of Tyre and Sidon. And, behold, a woman of Canaan *GENTILE* came out of the same coasts, and cried unto him, saying, Have mercy on me, O Lord, thou son of *JEWISH TERM* David; my daughter is grievously vexed with a devil. But he answered her not a word. And his disciples came and besought him, saying, Send her away; for she crieth after us. But he answered and said, I am not sent but unto the lost sheep of the house of Israel. Then came she and worshipped him, saying, Lord, help me. But he answered and said, It is not meet to take the children's bread, and to cast it to dogs. And she said, Truth, Lord: yet the dogs eat of the crumbs which fall from their masters' table. Then Jesus

answered and said unto her, O woman, great is thy
faith: be it unto thee even as thou wilt. And her
daughter was made whole from that very hour. (Matt.
15:21-28)

I grew up hearing this Scripture taught in Sunday school, but
I could never reconcile it with a loving, giving God. The
teachers had always told me how good God was, and how
generous He was to any who came to Him. Then they'd read
me this story and say the reason the woman received what she
wanted from the Lord was that she "hung in there," asking and
asking again, no matter how much it seemed like the Lord
made a meatball of her. It just didn't make sense to me that He
would act that way.

Years later, I heard someone teach what this message was
really all about. It fit together with what I knew to be true of a
loving God.

We can presume the woman had been watching Jesus heal
the sick, cast out devils, enable the blind to see, and perform
other miracles. In the midst of it all, she was hearing what the
people said as they came to Him. The Jews were saying, "Jesus,
thou Son of David, have mercy on me." That was a logical thing
for Jews to say. Not understanding what it was all about, the
woman memorized their approach and took it for her own.
She went up to Jesus and said, "Jesus, thou Son of David, have
mercy on me. My daughter is grievously vexed with a devil."

Jesus acted as if He didn't even hear her. That was
appropriate because what she was mouthing didn't represent
her true self to Him at all. It was a put-on, an approach
calculated to get what she wanted.

Silence is a tremendous tool, one of the things God uses
often in dealing with His people. Jesus said He'd never leave us
or forsake us, and He never does leave us, but He seems to
hide a lot. By His silence, He can pull a shade down over His

presence.

The purpose of the silence is to demand that we take inventory of ourselves. We see that something is out of position, something is out of line, something isn't right. And we know the fault is never with God; it's always with us.

The first mistake the woman made with Jesus was that she faked a relationship with Him, acting like a Jewess when she wasn't one at all. She was a Greek, a woman from the land of Canaan. She should have come saying, "Lord, I'm a stranger, but I'm bringing my problem to you." He'd have heard her because of her honesty from the very beginning.

As it was, Jesus didn't speak to her at first but said to His disciples, "You know, brethren, I'm sent only to the lost sheep of the house of Israel." That unmasked the woman and showed her that He knew she wasn't really Jewish and had no right to be speaking as if she was. When she realized that, she came out from behind the facade she had constructed. She became honest with the Lord and worshiped Him, saying, in essence, "Lord, it's me. Help me, Lord. How about just a crumb? Even the dogs are permitted the crumbs that fall from the table."

"Now that's what I call faith!" Jesus said. And He granted her request. As long as she approached Him in pretense, He paid no attention to her. She had to reach the point of total honesty in order to be able to receive what the Lord had to give her.

Our intercessions will fall short if our own relationship with God is not kept vital by personal prayer. Our first responsibility before God is to get ourselves in right relationship with Him; then we have something to give others. That's a universal law of priesthood—the preparation of the priest, then his ministry to the people.

God's people have settled too long for a general, unspecific prayer for themselves that goes something like this:

"Lord, I just come to you and ask you to forgive me for all the sins I've committed in the last twenty-four hours since I was here last to speak to you, and I pray that whatever needs to be done in me, you'll figure it out for yourself and do it. In Jesus' name, Amen."

Then we take off and go about our business, giving no more thought to prayer for ourselves. No wonder we're not growing! In the Book of James, Jesus says to us, "The reason you don't have more is because you don't ask. I want you to learn to ask me for what you need in order to grow up in my image." He's trying to bring us to new maturity levels so that we will pray more boldly and let Him accomplish more in us and through us. When we learn what His Word promises us, we can ask for it.

One day a mother and her five-year-old son sat down at the kitchen table to eat some soup for lunch. The child picked up his spoon and started stirring.

"Ask the blessing, Tommy," his mother reminded him.

He nodded, and kept on stirring his soup, looking intently at it, not saying anything.

"What *are* you doing?" his mother asked finally, her curiosity to the bursting point.

Tommy didn't raise his eyes as he answered, "It's alphabet soup, isn't it? I figured maybe God would make up the prayer."

That's about the level at which we're operating when we get down on our knees and all that comes out is, "Lord, I pray for my class, I pray for my home, I pray for me as a mother, as a PTA member, and as a car pool driver. Bless me and let your will be done in every aspect of my life. Amen."

I'm a great believer in specific prayers. And, much to my surprise, I have even learned to appreciate written prayers. When I was growing up in the Pentecostal movement, people always prayed just as the Lord gave them the words on the spot. There was never anything written down ahead of time. Whenever I saw people in other churches praying from words that were already written down, I thought they were somehow inferior. And I figured God didn't hear their prayers. But then He set things up to teach me something I needed to know.

There was a typist who used to come to my office early in the morning and do some typing for me before she went to her regular job. Every day, she prayed for me, typing out her prayer and putting it on my desk. The first thing I'd see when I walked into the office was a piece of paper that read something like this:

"Dear God, I bring Iverna before you this morning, and I ask you to work through her today to accomplish your will in the life of every person who comes into this office. I pray that you'll counsel through her with the wisdom of the Lord Jesus Christ. Provide everything she needs today, Lord. And don't let her have just a giving-out day. Let her receive blessings, too."

Can you imagine what it did to me to start my day reading that prayer? I'd rub my hands together and say, "O Lord! I'm ready to go. Thank you for hearing that prayer. Let's get on with this perfect day."

One of the beauties of the typist's written prayer was that it wasn't a generalized nothing prayer. It was specific, point by point, asking something in particular and expecting God to provide it.

A generalized prayer is usually an indication of a low level of faith. If we pray, "Lord, just bless the people tonight," when the meeting is over, we may be able to say, "I really believe people were blessed. I believe the Lord answered my prayer." But if we have gone out on a limb of faith, praying, "Lord, get ahold of Joan tonight, in Jesus' name," and have seen her dissolve in tears before the final amen, we can say, "Hallelujah! Look at how the Lord answered that one!" and our faith grows a mile.

We need to learn to pray specific prayers for ourselves so that our lives might be regulated by the Spirit of God, turning us into the living Word of God as we walk in His precepts. As we do so, the testimonies of the Lord become precious to us because walking in them, and appropriating them for ourselves, we find we have power with God. Power with God is better than money in a savings account.

"Pray for this child who has leukemia," someone says.

Ex. "Lord, I'm here in the name of Jesus Christ to withdraw a healing from your riches in glory on behalf of a little girl who needs it." With the power God has given us in prayer, we can receive from the resources of God.

Prayer is one of the greatest tools God has given His church. All through church history, prayer has broken the fetters of the enemy; prayer has released the power of the strong man over individual lives, over whole communities.

It used to be that a man or woman of faith would step into a place, take hold of a word from the Lord and say, "God, I believe you for the salvation of everyone in this factory." Almost overnight, whole shifts of people would be saved.

Today, we're more crisis-oriented. We learn of one person with an extreme need and encourage the whole congregation to concentrate on getting victory for that one. If the enemy can keep us crisis-oriented, he will prevent our growing to maturity. Crisis-oriented people don't see any need to pray for themselves when things are going well. Nor do they see any need for anyone else to intercede for them.

"I'm not having any trouble," they smile. Chances are they are not growing in the Lord, either. We should learn how to pray when there's not a crisis so we'll know how to pray when one comes.

Jabez was a man who prayed when things were not in crisis. His prayer, hidden in a long genealogy in 1 Chronicles, can teach us a lot about how we ought to pray for ourselves:

> And Jabez was more honourable than his brethren:
> and his mother called his name Jabez, saying,

Ex.

Because I bare him with sorrow. And Jabez called on the God of Israel, saying, <u>Oh that thou wouldest bless me indeed, and enlarge my coast, and that thine hand might be with me, and that thou wouldest keep me from evil, that it may not grieve me! And God granted him that which he requested.</u> (1 Chron. 4:9-10)

3

"Bless Me Indeed!"

Jabez began his prayer for himself by saying, "Oh that thou wouldest bless me indeed!" (1 Chron. 4:10).

We know very little about this man Jabez. He's mentioned in the Bible in only one place. His name means sorrowful, because his mother bore him in sorrow.

Many of the fruits of our own lives are birthed in sorrow. We cannot give spiritual birth to anyone; the Lord has to do that. But after someone has been born again of the Spirit of God, the Lord may put the baby in our laps for nurturing. That nurturing will usually bring some sorrow into our lives.

"You be the mother of this child," the Lord seems to say, and even if the child has the lineage of an Isaac, that doesn't mean it will be easy for us to bring him up in the way he should go. He won't necessarily want to learn the ways of God. The precepts of God will be foreign to him in the beginning, and the concepts of God will be totally lacking from his life. He may know only that up there somewhere is an ethereal being called God.

As we take a babe in Christ and try to share with him something of God and His truth, he may turn a deaf ear more times than not. God may have us on our knees in his behalf, weeping before the Lord day after day, maybe hours at a time, if He has really given us a burden for that soul. Sometimes we'll know the nature of our prayer for the individual; other times we'll be groaning in utterances that can't be put into words. And then one glorious day, we may see the child of God open himself to the fulness of the life of Christ in him. Chances are Jabez experienced similar things in his own ministry.

When Jabez cried out to God, "Oh that thou wouldest bless me indeed!" he was putting himself in line for three different kinds of blessing from God, blessings that in combination would fulfill the meaning of the word *indeed* which means "completely, wholly; entirely, and without reservation." That's the kind of blessing we need for our lives too.

The three different kinds of blessing include the blessing *of* the Lord, the blessing *from* the Lord, and the *further* blessing that enables us to be a blessing to others.

The blessing *of* the Lord is the blessing of His spiritual and temporal presence. He dwells in me, and I in Him. He is my God, and I am His. He walks with me, He talks with me, and He leads me wherever I go.

Christians frequently say to one another, "God bless you." One day I met a Christian from Australia who didn't say that, nor did he say simply, "Hello, how are you? I'm pleased to meet you." Instead, he looked me right in the eyes and said, "The blessing of the Lord be upon you, sister." I knew at once that he had an understanding of what he was saying to me, and suddenly I felt separated into a place of divine honor.

Many of us have been taught that the blessing *of* the Lord can be equated with a good, happy, funny feeling that comes from a spiritual church service, where each little goose bump produces a crop of its own.

"Oh, that was really the blessing of the Lord!" we might say. Maybe we saw God do something special in the service. The singing was probably lively. We felt like clapping our hands, dancing, or raising holy hands to the Lord.

Those things are fine, but the real blessing of the Lord is the presence of the Lord himself.

Moses knew about the blessing of the Lord. At one point in his life, God said to him, "Moses, you've got a lot of problems trying to lead this rebellious people. They have a lot of problems too. But go ahead and lead them, walking in faith, and I'll send some angels to go before you."

Most of us would have said, "Good deal, Lord. Thanks for the angels! That's all I'll need."

If God would say to me, "Iverna, I'm going to give you a mighty angel—your own personal guide—to walk before you where all shall see him," I'd be excited.

"Really, Lord?" I'd say. And I'd start thinking about how wonderful it would be for people to see me walking around with an angel in front of me. I'd imagine people exclaiming, "There she goes! That's Iverna and her angel."

But Moses had more sense than I do. Instead of telling God, "Good deal!" when God offered him guardian angels all over the place, Moses said, "If *your* presence doesn't go with me, God, I don't want to go."

Some Christians have come to the point in their own walk with the Lord where they can say, in all sincerity, "Lord, there is no exchange for your presence. I don't care about angels; I don't care about miracles; I don't care about anything unless I know you yourself are with me."

I've heard eloquent speakers who left me feeling empty and fruitless. I've heard faltering speakers who left me aware of the blessing and anointing of God because His presence was made manifest in them. There's no problem in deciding which we'd rather hear, the man who is speaking in his own ability or the man who is speaking with the blessing of the presence of the Lord.

The world is hungering, not for church or religion, not for

eloquent words. It is starved for life, a real life flow from God. Where the life flow is, the presence of the living Lord is. In the blessing of His presence, needs are met way beyond human expectations.

Every believer needs to understand he has been created to be the temple of the living God, enjoying the blessing of the Lord continually. When we sing, "Let the temple be filled with His glory!" we're asking for every believer to be filled with Him. There is no other blessing that can compare with the blessing *of* the Lord.

You are enjoying the blessing of the Lord when you go around walking and talking with Him, when you drive up to a stop sign and realize the driver of the car in the next lane is looking at you strangely, wondering if you're all there, because you seem to be talking to yourself.

In the midst of the blessing of the Lord, we may have to stop for a passenger train to cross the road. As it goes by, we pray for every passenger on it, for the conductor, the engineer, the dining room steward. . . .

"Lord, bless them and help them."

When we are experiencing the blessing of the Lord, in everything good that happens to God's children, our instant reaction is to say, "Thank you, Lord." If something bad happens to somebody, we're on our knees interceding, "Help them, Lord. Have mercy on them."

Far too often, the church doesn't even think about the blessing *of* the Lord. It settles for the blessing *from* the Lord. The blessing from the Lord includes the gift of the Holy Spirit and the power of the Holy Spirit working through His gifts of ministries to His church. It produces the fruit of the Spirit in our lives, and the temporal blessings He bestows just because we belong to Him. Such blessings are wonderful enough, but without the blessing *of* the Lord, they fall far short of what we ought to seek for ourselves.

God gives favor to men in lots of ways. The kind of life we sometimes take for granted is God's gift to us. If a man seems to be a natural salesman, and week after week he brings home a good paycheck, it could be that the favor he has with his boss and his customers is God's special gift to him, God's special blessing on his life. He is the One who puts us up; He is the One who puts us down.

The Bible says that in the last days young men will see visions. Meditating on this Scripture, I see hundreds of young men driving to work morning after morning, passing by a large field with a "For Sale" sign stuck up in the middle of it. One man says, "I see a prosperous service station on that field." He has a vision for the field, buys it, builds a service station, and has an immediately successful business there. Out of the hundreds of young men, he was the one who had a vision for what could be done with that field, and the Lord prospered him in it. That, too, was a blessing from the Lord.

<u>When a man's ways please the Lord, there's a blessing on all that he does and has and is. If poverty strikes, it behooves us to look at it and say, "All right, Lord, you've got my attention. What's going on? Where did I miss you? What are you saying to me in this?"</u>

If we're not yet that far along, we might begin by praying, "Lord, things aren't going very well for me just now. There are all these bills to pay, and I don't have anything with which to pay them."

At one time in my life, I was having some serious financial problems. Everything I did in the financial realm was wrong. At the time, a lady missionary was visiting my brother Judson who just happened to live across the street from me. One day my sister-in-law, Eleanor, came out of her house with the missionary. As they were standing on the sidewalk together, my sister-in-law said to the missionary, "When you think of Iverna, remember to pray for her. Things are awfully tough for

her financially. Ever since she's moved to Oregon, she's had
nothing but setbacks."

The woman reared back, as only lady preachers can do, and
shouted, "I rebuke the spirit of poverty! I bind the spirit of
poverty, and I command him to leave her door!"

"The spirit of poverty?" Eleanor said. "I didn't know there
was such a thing."

The missionary gave her a funny look and continued her
prayer.

For a while, things seemed to go a little bit better for me, and
I gave myself all the glory and praise for turning into such a wise
manager. Naturally, the Lord had to let me learn my lesson a
little better than that. I headed into a real "Operation
Stripdown" this time.

When we are His, and He is the Lord of our lives, He is
always providing all our needs, but there seem to be times
when the Lord has to strip us of material possessions to get our
attention. But being stripped avails us nothing unless we
return to the Lord in the circumstances.

"I've been trying to get your attention, child," He might say
to us. "There are some things we need to talk about."

God has let me go through the loss of all my material
belongings twice in my life in order for me to learn that He is
the owner, and I am the steward of all that He lets me use in
this life. After I had learned my lesson, He gave it all back to me
to enjoy. Now I say, "Lord, you have a lovely home here. I so
appreciate your letting me live in your lovely home." I drive
His car with pleasure, and eat at His banquet table, and I
never forget that it all belongs to Him.

The church has not brought glory to the Lord by
representing poverty and problems to the world. It will bring
glory to Him when it enjoys His abundance, shares it with
others, and proclaims that all the blessings come from God to
His children.

The blessing from the Lord, the gifts of the Holy Spirit, are given "without repentance," the Word tells us (Rom. 11:29).

Sometimes we see men and women with great ministries, people who have the gifts of the Spirit operating through them in mighty ways, but their own lives don't measure up. Somewhere along the line, their holiness and uprightness before God have fallen into pride and error. When the gifts continue to operate through such unclean vessels, we're often frustrated and confused.

"Why, God? Why do you continue to use such a person as he has become?"

"Because I never take back my gifts," He tells us. "They are given without repentance. I don't change my mind about the ones I call and the ones to whom I give blessing."

Some people think that when a gift is channeled to God's people through a vessel who has become impure or who has fallen into error that the power making the gift operational is from the devil. That's not true. The power is still from God who gave it to begin with.

Jesus said many would come in the last days and say to Him, "Lord, didn't we cast out devils in your name? Didn't we heal the sick? Didn't we prophesy in your name?" (Matt. 7:22).

The Lord will admit that they did these things in the power of His name, all right. They might have had successful ministries too, as the world looks at it. But their ministries were not attended with the blessing of the presence of the Lord. God may honor a ministry long after the vessel has fallen from grace. But the blessing *of* the Lord, not the blessing *from* the Lord, is what cleanses the vessel, making room for the flow of His life.

"Depart from Me, for I never knew *you*," Jesus will say to such persons (Matt. 7:23). The word *knew* here means "approval." The gifts of the Spirit are tools furnished by the Holy Spirit for ministry. But the gift as it comes forth is also mingled with something from the vessel. That's why we're to judge prophecy, and that's why we're to stay in close union with the Giver if we're going to have the gifts operating through us.

Et· If we have a problem with these things, we need to pray, "Lord, I'm sorry. I confess there is an ambitious spirit within me. It isn't really that I want the Word to be done so that your name alone will be glorified. I want to be seen, I want to be known, I want people to say, 'Just look at the power of God manifested in that life.' "

Et· Having confessed your sin, you can tell Him, "Lord, please cleanse me of this tendency toward self-exaltation. What I really want, Lord, is for your very own presence to go with me everywhere."

A searchlight is being focused on the downfall of widely known persons in order that all of us might recognize our responsibilities to walk in paths of righteousness and to learn to pray in faith for those brethren.

The third blessing for which Jabez was asking when he prayed, "Oh that thou wouldest bless me indeed!" was the blessing of being a blessing.

Et "Lord, make me a blessing" doesn't mean, "O Lord, let me make somebody happy today." It means, "Lord, produce your life in me, so that every time I speak, I will produce life in others."

In order to be a blessing to others, we have to graduate from the desire to be important, to have the attention of the people and inspire them by virtue of our personality.

"I enjoyed it," people used to say to me after a service. "Real entertaining. You've got lots of humor in your message—makes it fun to listen to and easy to remember."

That used to please me, but then God got ahold of me, and I got ahold of Him in a more mature way.

Ex "O God, I don't want to be an entertainer!" I cried. "I want to be a *blessing*! I don't want just to make people laugh—I want them to see your life flowing through me and receive it for themselves. I don't want the focus to be on my name. I want to lift up the name of Jesus so He can transform lives. I want to be your instrument for giving people living water so they won't have to thirst again. I want to stir up faith in others, to let the deliverance that has restored life in me bring that Life to them. I want to do a lasting work. I want the life that you minister through me to remain."

Abraham knew what it was to be a blessing. God had said to him, "In blessing, I will bless thee" (Gen. 22:17). I used to read that and think it was some kind of double-talk. There was no way I could figure it out. And then I realized God was saying, "Abraham, I will enable you to be a blessing to other people. And through your blessing others, I will bless you." This is what I've come to call the blessing of usefulness.

Next to the blessing of the Lord—the blessing of His presence—the blessing of usefulness is one of the greatest blessings God gives to His people.

During the years when I worked as a counselor, one of the most tragic things I found among people was a sense of uselessness, a feeling that no one needed them for anything. There is nothing on earth more devastating than uselessness. The slum areas of big cities are infested with the derelicts of society—well-educated personalities, sometimes professional and business people—who have come to a place in their lives where they say, "Nobody needs me; nobody wants me," and they turn to the bottle and drink their lives away.

Young people and senior citizens alike, and all the ages in between, need to have a sense that someone, somewhere, needs them, that they can produce what is lacking in the life of another. God created us with a desire to be useful, and He says, "If my blessing is upon a life, and within a life, in that blessing I will bless you by using you. I will multiply you. You will get sons and daughters who will receive a blessing through you and who will, in turn, share the blessing with others."

True usefulness isn't just listening to other people pour out

their problems; it's ministering to their needs by the power
that is within you.

For years before I understood this, I was a good spiritual
garbage can. I had a good tight lid, could hold a lot, and had
sense enough to pour it all out to the Lord often enough that it
didn't overflow and contaminate the whole community around
me. I didn't blab what was told me in confidence; I didn't act
like the neighborhood gossip, but I emptied it all before the
Lord as I interceded for the persons with the awful problems.
In the meantime, they were out getting full of garbage again.
The result was a never-ending cycle, but I was deceived into
thinking I was blessing the family of God.

One day it dawned on me that I was hearing the same people
over and over again, that they were still talking about the same
old problems, pouring out the same collection of garbage day
after day, week after week. Whatever "good" I did them was
terribly short-lived.

"God, there's got to be an answer!" I cried out to Him. "This
getting nowhere is getting me down."

"In blessing I will bless thee," He seemed to say. "If you get
enough of me down inside and you begin to minister my life to
them, there can be a healing, there can be a change in them."

The *real* blessing of usefulness is not to be found in the
exercise of the gifts and talents the Lord has given us but in the
flow of His life through us. We might come to a day when the
so-called usefulness that came from the work of our hands or
our talent for preaching, singing, or whatever, just doesn't
seem to bring blessing to people any more.

"What happened, Lord?"

"I'm shaking anything that can go. The only thing I want to
have left is pure gold."

"Then how can I bless people, Lord?"

"Only by letting my life flow through you to touch their lives.
No other way."

Some ministers are finding this out today—the hard way. They're preaching about like they used to, scheduling the same number of potluck suppers, but instead of drawing the crowds, they're driving them away. Their churches are deserted. Empty pews stare back at them Sunday after Sunday. The ministers are completely baffled.

"I don't understand what I'm doing wrong!" they wail to anyone who will listen.

It's not that they're doing anything wrong; the program is just as good as it's ever been. It's just that they're not doing enough of what is right—spending real time in prayer so that God can run His church through them the way He wants to do it.

When God blesses others through you, He always blesses you at the same time. Furthermore, He says He will also turn it around: "I will bless those who bless you!" (Gen. 12:3, RSV). There's nothing better than an arrangement of that kind: I bless you; you bless me. God blesses you for blessing me and He blesses me for blessing you. We all win.

Sometimes people say, "Oh, if the words would only roll out of me like they do out of you when you preach, I'd be so thrilled." Others say, "Oh, if I could sing like Shirlee can sing," or "If I could communicate to the deaf in sign language like JoAnne can—"

Everyone can see the beauty of the blessing coming through another life. But it's time for us to recognize that the smallest talent in us, the faintest smile from us, can start an endless circle of blessing.

Paul said we're not to measure our Christian lives against one another, trying to prove we're more spiritual than our neighbor. We are to measure our spirituality only with reference to the standard set by Jesus.

It's not good for us to compare ourselves with others.

God and I

"If I could just be like so-and-so. If I could pray like this one, and sing like that one, and understand the Word like the other one—"

Feeling that we fall short, we might wind up doing nothing but lamenting our relative imperfections and shortcomings. We need to see that God has made each of us to be unique. Not one of us is supposed to be a carbon copy of another human being.

In the old days, the longing in my heart was not to be like Jesus but to be like my brother Judson. I held that man in such high esteem—he was so eloquent in his delivery of the Word; he could impart the Scripture like a theologian; yet he had a tender heart toward the people. Judson never made the dumb, bumbling mistakes that I did, frustrating people.

"Lord, if I could only become as smooth as Judson," I used to pray, thinking that if I dogged his footsteps long enough, I might become a little more like him. We worked together for ten years, and at the end of that time, I looked at both of us and realized I could never mirror him, no matter how hard I tried. At the same time, the Lord spoke to my heart and said, "That's right, Iverna. But if you'll stop trying to pattern your life and ministry after Judson's, in time you *will* mirror me."

Many people have the idea that if the Lord wants to bless them, He'll go ahead and do it without their asking. "And if He doesn't want to bless me," they say, "well, that's all right, too. I'll just go on praising Him anyhow." But the Bible says we are to ask, and Jabez was obedient to this command. He wanted blessing, so he asked for it and got it.

I have prayed the same prayer Jabez prayed, asking God to bless me indeed. In the natural, it would be quite impossible for a divorcee traveling in the ministry to be prosperous, and have joy, peace, happiness, life, and victory in Jesus, but I have these things because I've asked God to bless me. Without His blessing, I have learned I am less than nothing.

When I first began to venture out into the blessings God had for me, I was so timid that I just tiptoed into the edge of the water. But before long, I learned to venture out into the deep, confident that He would uphold me.

Everything went along fine with me for a while, just as it did for Abraham. But then one day, something was required of him. God said, "Abraham, do you really love your son Isaac?"

"Love Isaac? Lord, I never dreamed I could even *have* a child, and Isaac is *such* a wonderful child! He's so fair, so beautiful, so obedient—exactly what you promised. He is the seed from which your blessing is to come forth, and he's such a joy to Sarah and to me—"

"Good," the Lord said. "Now I want you to take him for a walk and sacrifice him on an altar to me."

When Abraham had laid the boy on the altar, Isaac had a question for him. "Dad, this is probably a dumb question, but what's going on? I mean, where's the sacrifice? I hope it's not what it looks like—"

"Son, God will provide the sacrifice," Abraham told him.

Even when he had the knife raised in his hand, ready to plunge it into the breast of his promised son, Abraham still believed the promise of God that many nations would come forth from Isaac.

There may come a time in our lives when God will say, "Take the blessing I have given you, and lay it on the altar. Take a knife and slay the thing that you love."

"No, God!" we scream in protest.

"Why do you have difficulty in making the offering?" God might ask us. "Don't you know that everything you have came from me? It grieves me that you would hold back, because you should know that if I ask you for something, it is only that I might give you something better."

Abraham didn't seem to have this kind of problem. He was ready to kill his son, not because he was some super-spiritual maniac, but because he had faith that God's promise would be kept. Isaac's conception and birth had been a miracle from the beginning. Abraham could believe God would perform another miracle—a miracle of resurrection—to restore life to him.

We're not to hang on to our blessings with a tenacity that says, "God, I could never let you have this."

God might say, "Of course you can't let me have it; I already own it. Everything you think you have is really mine."

Isaac was a man of faith and prayer just as his father had been. But from the day of their birth, Isaac's sons looked rotten and impossible. Jacob was a cheating, deceiving, conniving young man who wanted the blessing and the birthright. He managed to get the birthright by cheating Esau, and when he wanted the blessing that went with it, his mother said, "Don't worry, son. I'll help God give that to you."

As Jacob went on through life, people treated him as badly as he had treated others. When his uncle Laban cheated him, Jacob didn't put up a big fight, because he knew he had it coming to him.

But God wasn't interested in evening the score; He was interested in fulfilling His promise of blessing to Abraham, Isaac, and Jacob. And in order to get them ready to receive the thing He had promised, He had to get their lives in order.

Why do we think it should be any different with us? Why do we pray, "Lord, bless me indeed," and then scream at God's dealings with us as He prepares us to be vessels able to receive and contain the blessings He has in store for us?

At one point in Jacob's life, he had a divine encounter with God. There was a vision of angels ascending and descending a stairway from earth to heaven (Gen. 28:12), and the Lord standing beside him and promising to make him and his descendants a blessing (Gen. 28:13-14). And finally, there was the Son of God himself, wrestling all night with Jacob.

Toward morning, Jacob confessed what had been birthed in

his heart:

"I will not let you go until you bless me" (Gen. 32:26, paraphrased).

Hosea 12:4 tells us that Jacob had power over the angel. He wept and sought God's favor and he prevailed. His prayer was answered.

Why is it that instead of struggling all night with God, we offer Him just five minutes of prayer to do a work? We pray, "Lord, today I bring to you this church, and I pray you'll stir the pastor. I pray you'll work with the assistant. Be with the leaders of the church. Please stir them up too. Let there come a mighty move in Jesus' name. Amen."

We pray it once, then wait. As the months go by, we complain, "I don't know what it is. I guess God isn't interested in blessing **our** church."

But Jacob fought for what he wanted. And the Lord said, "I'll let you prevail because of your importunance, your perseverance. And I'll give you a little sign to help you remember this night." He touched Jacob in the hollow of his thigh, and every limping step Jacob took from that time on reminded him that God was the one who had *really* prevailed. He wanted to get Jacob to the place where He *could* bless him.

He wants to get us to the same place. And the Great Commission is a blessed privilege that God has given the church. That commission says to us all, "Come on! You've got a purpose to live for, every one of you. I've given you the power to witness, the power to be the salt of the earth, the power to be light wiping out darkness, and I tell you, 'You *are* my disciples.'"

There is extreme teaching about "discipleship" making the rounds today that has made some people afraid to believe that we are disciples. When Paul said, "Be ye followers of me, even as I also am of Christ" (1 Cor. 11:1), he was saying to the people, "You don't know Jesus as well as I know Him, so watch me, and I'll reveal Him to you." That's the way in which we are to understand the business of making disciples; we're to help people become disciples of Jesus, not of ourselves. Even the Holy Spirit doesn't teach about himself, but He always reveals Jesus. The blessing of usefulness to which our Lord has called us all is the blessing of His life being lived in us and poured out from us.

4

"Who Shall Stand?"

Many of us have ascended the hill of the Lord. We have known what it is to come into that holy place where we knew we were in the presence of Jesus, enjoying the blessing *of* the Lord. Oh, what sweet communion! What fellowship we had with Him there!

But afterward, we always descended. Getting into the presence of the Lord is one thing; abiding there, standing there with Him, is something else. Sometimes we get sick and tired of ascending and descending, ascending and descending. We yearn to stay in His presence forever, and we wonder how we can accomplish it.

We find the Psalmist asking some questions relevant to our wonderings:

> Who shall ascend into the hill of the Lord? or who shall stand in his holy place? (Ps. 24:3)

When the Psalmist asked the questions, he received some answers. The Bible gives us some clear keys to remaining in the kingdom of God. But if we don't know how we got there in the first place, we won't know how to get there again.

"I don't know how I got there. It just happened. I was just sitting there in the prayer meeting, praising Him, and suddenly, WHOOSH! I just soared right up into the holy place. The Lord was there all right, and I just kept bowing and dancing and singing and praising Him. It was glorious!"

"Why didn't you stay there if it was so good?"

"Oh, man, I couldn't have *lived* if I had stayed there. The diet was too rich. I had to come back down."

"What are you trying to do now?"

"Oh, I'm trying to get back up there, of course. I'm trying to climb up the hill."

"That's all of us, Lord. You take us there by your Spirit, and then we struggle to climb back up in our own strength. It's no wonder that we fail. Forgive us, Lord, for ever thinking we could do what you alone can accomplish. Lord, please take me back up the hill."

The next verses in the psalm reveal the one who is able to stand.

> He that hath clean hands, [blameless, innocent, guiltless hands] and a pure heart; who hath not lifted up his soul unto vanity, nor sworn deceitfully. (Ps. 24:4)

The word "hands" is speaking about external actions, the things that we do. If we do what is right and refrain from doing what is wrong, our hands will be clean. We'll have met one qualification for coming to the hill of God—the continual blessing *of* the Lord—and remaining there.

A pure heart is a second qualification. The word used for "pure" in this Scripture means *empty*. A pure heart is one that is empty of ourselves, empty of our problems, empty of everything else so that it might be filled to capacity with God.

One who has not lifted up his soul to vanity nor sworn deceitfully is one who is not guilty of pretense, insincerity, or falsehood. Any one of these traits can destroy us and make us desolate.

The one who would stand in His holy place must have purity of outward actions reflecting that inward holiness of attitude which is a work of grace.

Today we don't find as many wrong attitudes among God's people as we find careless actions. A person acting in sin, someone with dirty hands, seldom tries to defend his sin as a right action. Usually he will admit his hands are dirty.

"I know I'm not doing right, but—" Then he continues with something like, "The Lord knows my frame is dust. He understands my weakness, and He knows my needs."

Another person might confess, "I know I ought to ask so-and-so to forgive me, but I just can't bring myself to do it."

Such persons, being deliberately disobedient to God's Word, will not be able to stand on the holy hill. They'll have to keep climbing up and down, ascending and descending, having to be satisfied with a little splash-over of glory resulting from the clean hands and pure hearts of the rest of the congregation. They will not be able to remain in the presence of the Lord when the meeting is over. They'll tremble all the way to the parking lot, walking carefully, afraid they'll lose the blessing before they find their car. The minute such persons walk out of a service in which God's people have been fed and nourished by His presence, they'll feel the old, hollow emptiness gnawing at them again. Maybe they'll grumble a little, not understanding what has happened.

"I don't know how people can say they're *always* walking in the presence of the Lord. It doesn't happen to *me* like that."

No wonder.

It takes practice to remain sensitive to the continual presence of the Lord. But after we've reached that point, we may cry for more, just as Moses did:

"Lord, now that I'm walking with you, show me your glory!" (Exod. 33:18, paraphrased).

This is the cry of the church today, the bride awaiting the return of her bridegroom. She's no longer satisfied with just praising Him from Zion, she wants to be married to Him and dwell with Him all the time in an intimate relationship on His holy hill.

The voice of the bridegroom answers her by saying, "You can have this relationship with me, not because of your much praying and supplicating, but because your hands are clean and your heart is pure."

We pay a terrible price when we are unwilling to abide by His conditions, unwilling to wash our hands, unwilling to cleanse our lives of all wrongdoing. We pay the price of self-acceptance, for one thing, because we hate ourselves more for disobeying God than for any other thing. We pay the price of constant warfare too, not only with ourselves but with the world. On the other hand, when our ways please the Lord, He makes even our enemies to be at peace with us (Prov. 16:7).

I've seen a confirmation of this in my own life. A few years ago, I was having problems in certain areas, and I could see that I was making enemies I didn't need.

"O God," I prayed, "if my ways aren't pleasing to you, please reveal to me what I'm doing wrong."

"Keep your eyes on me, Iverna, and your mouth on me, too, and we'll get along just fine. Your ways will please me exactly, and I'll take care of your problems and your enemies for you, just as I've promised in my Word."

When I came into obedience, I saw Him do it. By His sovereign grace He performed miracle after miracle, restoring friendships that had been broken.

This is no day for the church to be separated, broken to

pieces, and grieving. It's a day for the generation that seeks the Lord to be prepared to *stand* on the holy hill.

Once upon a time, most of us were crisis-oriented. We had been saved, filled with the Holy Spirit, healed in our bodies and minds, and we thought that was all there was to it. So we went out and brought in someone else to be saved, filled, and healed. The next day, they went out with us, and we each brought in two more. Believers were being multiplied. It was wonderful. But today God's people are no longer satisfied with that. Instead of being content with the status quo, they're like a bride who is crying out, "Make me ready for the wedding! Get rid of all my spots and wrinkles and blemishes like you said you would!"

He's hearing that cry and doing something about it. Many Christians are being surprised at what they hear themselves praying. They might hear God's will for themselves in the words that come from their own mouths.

"O God, purge me! Make me whiter than snow!"

"I hear that prayer, daughter."

About then, the pray-er has had some second thoughts. She wants to grab the words and cram them back down, but God has heard them, so she has to settle for modifying the prayer a little bit.

"Please don't purge me of everything all at once, Lord. Do it just a little bit at a time."

I can imagine the Lord saying to the keeper of the heavenly warehouse, "Gabriel, do we have half a purge up here anywhere?"

When all this seeking after holiness began, I kept hearing preachers proclaim, "Jesus is coming soon. Maybe tomorrow."

Instead of rejoicing and joining my voice with those who were crying out, "Yes, Lord. Come quickly. Come quickly, Lord Jesus," I was wanting Him to wait a minute. And I thought He would wait because He knew what shape I was in. I was sure He wouldn't take me, and hell wouldn't have had me either. I'd have been stuck somewhere in between, and I didn't believe in purgatory. The whole situation seemed kind of iffy as far as my personal destiny was concerned. And so my prayers grew more fervent.

"Cleanse me, O God, and know my thoughts. See if there is still some wicked way in me, and if you find any, clean it out. O God, I don't want to have to keep coming to you day after day, month after month, year after year, with the same old garbage in my life. I want to be made ready to *stand* on your holy hill."

Why did other people and I begin to pray such a prayer? Why did we ask God to clean us up, to perfect us, and to make us more like Jesus all of a sudden? We'd had years when we *could* have been praying that way, but it hadn't entered our heads—or our hearts. The time has come, however, for the Holy Spirit to get the bride ready for the bridegroom. The Holy Spirit is the one who changed the nature of our prayers, so He could deck us with the ornaments of the bride, the graces of the nature and attributes of God, that we might be presented to Him, unblemished.

"Here's your bride, Son. Isn't she beautiful?"

If Jesus came today, He wouldn't find a beautiful bride; He'd find one carved up into segments, divided up by jealousies and unforgiveness. He's waiting for us to be made ready, whole and entire.

The ones who take the trouble to have clean hands and pure hearts, not lifting their souls to vanity nor swearing deceitfully, are the ones who will "receive the blessing from the Lord, and righteousness from the God of their salvation. This is the generation of them who seek him . . ." (Ps. 24:5-6, paraphrased).

The Scripture is saying that the seekers are the ones who will receive the blessing of the Lord, and they'll enjoy a righteous life from the God of their salvation, remaining on His holy hill.

The generation in which we live is surely the generation of those who seek Him. Looking back through church history, we don't find *generations* seeking Him, only a few people here and there. Today, almost every denomination has members who are seeking the Lord. Prayer groups are rising up even in churches that seem to know nothing of the Holy Spirit. One day the people of such churches are going to be on their knees, and they'll hear themselves pray, without understanding, "Give me more of you, Lord." He'll say, "I hear that prayer," and fill them with His Holy Spirit.

It's not by our many hours of prayer that we prove to the Lord that we're seeking Him. It's important to understand that, because some people think they can't seek the Lord at all if they don't have hours and hours every day when they can be on their knees.

A woman I knew came every morning to a prayer meeting at the church. That bothered her husband.

"It's not fair," he complained. "You get so much out of your praying, you're leaving me in the dust. I can see your spiritual life zooming forward way ahead of mine, and *I'm* supposed to be the spiritual head of our home. But I don't have the time to spend in prayer that you do."

When the woman reported all this to me, I asked her to send her husband in for a conference.

"I'm going to make you a promise," I told him. "If you will give God the time you *do* have, you will grow as rapidly as your wife is growing with her two hours a day. Tell me your schedule."

He told me when he went to work, what time he got home, and what his other time-consuming responsibilities were. I was impressed. No doubt about it, he was one *busy* young man. But there was one opening.

"Are you willing to get up thirty minutes early so you can

spend that much time with the Lord before you leave for work in the morning?"

"Yes, but that will have to include my Bible reading as well as my prayer time—"

"God knows the circumstances," I assured him. "He won't think you're cheating Him. Can you try this program for two months, using half the time speaking to God and the other half listening to what He has to say to you through His Word?"

He agreed to try it, and something tremendous happened. God opened the Word to him in such a mighty way that his whole life was changed. Today, he's a minister of the gospel himself.

It's not the *amount* of time we spend seeking God that matters; it's the quality of the time we spend in His presence. If we know we could spend two hours with Him and if we choose to cheat Him of all but a niggardly fifteen minutes, we'll get about an eighth of the blessing we would otherwise receive. But if all we have is fifteen minutes, and we give that to Him wholeheartedly, our cup will run over.

The Word tells us that we are to seek first the kingdom of God and His righteousness; and then everything else we need will be thrown in for good measure (Matt. 6:33).

Why should we seek the righteousness of God? Because the world has none of its own to offer. Unrighteousness is so widespread, we've come to expect it everywhere. We've been trained to distrust most of what we hear and half of what we see with our own eyes.

For example, I expect to be lied to by every automobile salesman. If I walk into a salesroom, I might ask the salesman, "How much is this automobile worth?"

"Well, it's easily worth $4,000, but I'll let *you* have it for $3,500. Best car on the lot."

"Probably really worth only $2,000," I tell myself. "And it'd fall apart before I could get it home."

That's terrible, but that's how our minds are conditioned to work these days.

We think we can't even trust Christians to be honorable. Even when it's all down on paper in legal language, properly notarized, we're afraid the other guy will try to squirm out of his part of the bargain.

I was taking a tour recently in Philadelphia, and the guide was dishing out some American history as we walked along.

"Years ago, our forefathers hardly ever signed anything," he said. "They'd just come to an agreement and shake hands on it. Their word was their bond, perfectly dependable. They did this in business, in professions, and in the government."

As I listened to the guide talk about how things were in the "good old days," my spirit cried out, "O God, if only life could be right, if only life could be fair, if only life could be righteous! If only I could say, 'Brother, I will,' and he could know, 'She said she would, and she will,' what a wonderful world this would be. I'd like to live in that kind of world."

"You're going to live in that kind of a world," the Holy Spirit reminded me. "When He shall reign as King of kings and Lord of lords, His will will be done on earth as it is in heaven—honesty, fairness, and truth will be everywhere in that perfect kingdom."

People who have engaged in wrong actions will not stand on the holy hill unless they become new creatures in Christ Jesus, wiping all the past away.

A lot of people today are trying to take care of the bad things in their past by going to psychiatrists or taking part in encounter groups, sensitivity groups, and group therapy sessions designed to help them know themselves. I'm not condemning such efforts, but I've found they're generally fruitless. The last thing likely to happen as a result of them is

47

real self-discovery. And if persons *do* discover themselves, they are doubly discouraged, because no amount of introspection can make right what is wrong with them.

What most people learn from such groups can be summed up in the remark one woman made when she had been attending therapy sessions for several months. "Well, I've learned that I have even more problems than I thought I had when I started. But that's all right. I'm not alone. Everybody else has 'em too."

Awareness that we have problems and that the rest of the world has them too does not have to lead to despair. Admittedly, the very act of digging into self has built-in seeds of frustration and futility, because we can't change ourselves. But for the believer, there's a different outlook. God knows our hearts are deceitful and desperately wicked, but He is able to change us. As God reveals us to ourselves, we can look at Him as in a mirror reflecting His glory and be changed from one degree of glory to another, from light to light, from revelation to revelation. God reveals things to us about ourselves by degrees, as soon as we can handle the knowledge and cooperate with His Holy Spirit to bring about a change.

We've all had the experience of having a thing revealed to us—perhaps a character defect—and thinking that was all that was wrong with us. When that particular failure had been cleared up by the Holy Spirit working in us, we shouted, "Hallelujah! I'm so glad to be rid of my defect." We thought we were pure and spotless then, without wrinkle or blemish. But then the Lord gently called to our attention something else that had to go.

"*Two* defects! I can't believe it!" But we came to believe it and found there were not just two things but more like two hundred and twenty-two things wrong with us. When the Lord had finished cleansing us of that many, a new batch of defects cropped up from somewhere. Becoming more and more like Jesus proved to be a lifetime thing.

In the church in which I grew up, we thought we didn't need God to make us holy. "We can figure it out for ourselves," we told Him. And we let our hair grow long and piled it in beehives on top of our heads; we fixed our faces to look worse than they did naturally, patting on ghostly powder and steering clear of the alive-looking lipstick. We carried our Bibles everywhere—big ones—advertising our testimony.

The world looked on, pointed a finger, and snickered, "Look there, children. That's what *not* to be."

But then came the sovereign outpouring of the Holy Spirit on all flesh. We saw His sons and daughters begin to prophesy, His old men to dream dreams, His young men to have visions, and as the Spirit opened our eyes to what was real, we repented.

"But Lord, we were only trying to be holy," we said, by way of excuse.

"I never told you to make yourselves holy," He reminded us. "I said you would *be* holy. I'm the only one who can make you holy." True holiness is made of the presence of the Lord, not of particular hair styles, make-up, or the absence of make-up. In His presence, we didn't have to ponder what was right and what was wrong. The light of His presence showed everything for what it was.

Today, God's people are in a crucible. The fire has been turned up under the pot, and we can feel the big scoop of the Holy Spirit as it reaches down and skims off the scum that's boiled up to the surface through God's dealings with us. A number of years ago, we were thrilled when we began to hear about how God was dealing with His people. We all began to pray, "O God, deal with me too." And He heard that prayer.

Today, many of us are crying, "O my God, what are you doing to me? Why are you letting these awful things happen to me?"

"I'm only answering your prayer," He tells us. And when we

God and I

think about it, we realize that the negatives that have been happening in our lives *have* been God's instruments for ridding us of dross, and more and more of that which remains in us is beginning to resemble pure gold. We're being made ready to stand on that holy hill.

When I asked the Lord to fill me with the Holy Spirit, it was glorious, but I didn't know what I was in for. At first, I felt like hanging from the chandeliers. I spoke in unknown tongues and thoroughly enjoyed the whole thing.

But later, as I was walking along, doing the things I had always done, something down inside me seemed to push a button that shouted, "Reject!"

"Hey, who are you?" I hollered.

"I'm the Lord's attorney, here to protect His interest in His temple," the indwelling Holy Spirit answered me. "You can't do that particular thing any more."

All my unsaintly carnal nature was aroused to indignation.

"What do you mean, I can't do that? I've been doing it for forty years."

"I know it, but that's all over now. This is the end of that in your life."

"But I'm a free moral agent, Holy Spirit."

"Not any more, you're not. You asked to have the Comforter come into your life, and here I am. I'm supposed to do my job, and I tell you, you won't be comfortable if you persist in wrong behavior."

"Well, then, I hereby relieve you of your duties, Comforter. I'm glad to have you in my life, but I'm asking you to stay dormant inside me because I still want to do what *I* want to do."

"Are you certain?"

"Absolutely."

"All right. Have it your way, but you won't like it."

And I didn't like it. Talk about leanness of soul! I knew all the misery of Jonah. I found that there's no sliding to backsliding; it's walking backward, uphill all the way. Everybody around

50

me looked happy, but I was miserable doing my own thing because I'd had a taste of the light.

The Holy Spirit within me let me know how He felt about it all.

"This repels me. I hate it, don't you?" He needled me.

I had to be honest with Him. Besides, He already knew the answer.

"Yeah, I hate it too," I admitted. "But I want to like it." I had already passed the point of no return, and I gradually became aware that the world would never have the same allure for me again. Nothing short of the glory to which you have been exposed can ever satisfy you again, no matter how much you pretend, no matter how hard you try.

I had to return to the Lord on a full commitment basis.

Since then, I have sometimes been in services I felt were as dry as dust, services where the leader, tears of joy streaming down his face, would stand up and cry, "Oh, the Spirit of the *Lord* is in this place!" People around me had visible goose bumps, and they were saying, "Oh, glory! Isn't this gorgeous!" But I felt nothing.

The enemy squatted on my shoulder and whispered to me, "Aren't you ashamed of yourself? You've lost all sensitivity to the Spirit of God, Iverna."

He used to be able to bring me under condemnation, but I've come to see what's really involved. The reality is that of *course* I was bored with what was happening in that service because the level of the Spirit's presence there was no more than what I was accustomed to walking in day by day. Why, I got up in the morning with that much blessing and anointing. No wonder the service didn't strike me as spectacular. I was longing for more of the presence of the Lord than that. He was calling me up higher.

Sometimes I look around and see that God's people are

completely unprepared for any tribulation which could come. They can barely stand on the hill of God now, during a time when the blessing of the Lord is being poured out on them, when rivers of life are flowing all about them. In the midst of what looks like health and prosperity, they are shaking their heads and crying, "Yes, I know the blessing of the Lord now, but—O God, help me!—I don't know about tomorrow."

If we fear our faith and love can be shaken, we should examine the foundation on which it is built. If our foundation is the rock, Jesus, we cannot be shaken by all the powers of hell. When we really know that, we might even come to the place where we will welcome the shaking of everything as a kind of vibrating spiritual rubdown that will feel great to us.

5

"Enlarge My Coast"

After Jabez had asked God to bless him indeed, he prayed that the Lord would enlarge his coast. The word "coast" here means "boundary, territory, area." "Enlarge" means to increase in every respect. Jabez was asking God to enlarge his territory, to increase it in every way.

It is time for all of God's people to have their coasts increased. This enlarging begins with an enlargement of our hearts. The prophet Isaiah spoke about heart enlargement.

> Lift up your eyes round about you and see. . . . You shall see and be radiant, and your heart shall thrill and tremble with joy, and be enlarged. (Isa. 60:4-5, TAB)

In the Old Testament, the word *heart,* as it is used here, refers to our will, our intellect, and our feelings. When God enlarges our hearts, He increases our whole being. We begin to see what He is doing; we begin to appropriate the promises of God.

There needs to be a blessing of enlargement upon every

ministry represented in the body of Christ. That means that every ministry will have to be cleansed.

God is trying to get all His people to a place where they will desire perfection in their own lives, praying, "Lord, I've got a lot of head knowledge of your will. Bring my life now to the level of that knowledge. Let me begin to really walk in your ways so that I might have an enlarged ministry to your glory."

I have had to pray that for my own life. For a time, God let me get by with almost anything, but one day He brought me up short.

"How about filling the gap, Iverna? Either bring your ministry down to the level where you're living, or let me bring your life up to the level where you're ministering."

"Lord, it would be a lot easier for me to bring my ministry down to the level of my life, wouldn't it?" I asked Him.

"Just how much life do you think you're living now?" He challenged me. Right away, I saw I'd better choose to let Him change me.

The Lord is constantly trying to bring all of us up higher. He is saying, "Do you really want to be a blessing? Do you really want to be able to help people? Then let me enlarge your coast. Let your whole life mature to higher levels than you've yet known."

We're supposed to check the level of the oil of the Holy Spirit in us just as we check the oil levels in our automobiles by putting in the dipstick. If the oil is low, maybe we need another quart of Holy Spirit before we try to show anyone else how to run the race.

There have not been any great earthshaking revelations to the body of Christ for some time. We've been given years to appropriate what He has shown us already. I sense that He is ready to reveal something to us again, but first we've got to walk in what He's already told us. We have to be obedient, and we also have to be willing to learn.

God doesn't argue with us to show us we don't have all the answers; He just holds the laver up. The laver is the basin the priests looked into every time they were preparing to enter the Holy of Holies. The water in the laver reflected the priest's image back to him.

One day when I took a look in God's laver, I thought, "My God! I thought I looked better than that!"

"I know," He said gently. "That's why I'm letting you have a look."

I got back in the Word for my cleansing.

A traveling minister has a better opportunity to stagnate than other ministers. Because I have a briefcase full of messages God has given me in the past, I could minister without ever opening the Bible again. Many people can't detect the difference between fresh bread and stale bread. But I praise God that He puts a stirring inside us that says, "I want to hear daily from God. I want to get ahold of the Lord today for today. I want my knowledge of Him to be increased so He can make me a blessing."

When we pray that God will enlarge our coasts, we're asking that our prejudices, fears, and all other negative factors in us might be removed, that we might flow with the Spirit and reach beyond ourselves in concern for others.

My generation has a hang-up the next one doesn't have. I grew up in the time of the Latter Rain movement which, in its inception, was a true visitation of God. But unfortunately, it wasn't always coupled with knowledge on the part of the people, and in some places, it went off the deep end. People weren't willing to seek knowledge; they just wanted to enjoy their feelings. The flow of love was so great, they went all the way over into free love. The flow of prophecy was so beautiful, nobody bothered to check it out. People acted as if they didn't care what spirit was behind it all, and so they fell for a lot of things that were not of God. As a result, His outpouring was continued upon only a remnant—the mature Christians who walked in the light of His Word as the Spirit gave understanding.

The excesses were so extreme, that afterward, every time God began to move sovereignly, people would warn us, "Better be careful about moving with the Spirit, because it's so easy to be deceived. Just look at what happened to the Latter Rain people." Fear of the counterfeit kept some from seeking God's real presence.

Misunderstanding of love doesn't mean that love is unreal. We are commanded to love, but we are to love within the will of God. Misuse of prophecy doesn't mean that prophecy has to go. We are not to despise prophesying (1 Thess. 5:20), but we are to check it out. When we follow the scriptural precautions, we can move out in freedom without fear, and we do not have to quench the Spirit.

The first time I raised one hand in praising the Lord, it weighed five hundred pounds. And I thought our church had been led into demon activity when a woman came and taught our young people to dance before the Lord. But when I got my Bible out, thinking the best way to deal with her was through the Word of God, *I* got dealt with instead. The Word said, "Let them praise his name in the dance" (Ps. 149:3). Much to my surprise, I learned that dancing before the Lord is highly recommended. God spoke through the prophet, saying, "Behold, I will do a new thing; now it shall spring forth" (Isa. 43:19).

That prophecy has been fulfilled in every preceding generation, and it is now being fulfilled in ours.

Some denominational churches preached that this new thing was going to happen. But when it began to happen all around them, they stood still, not letting their own coasts be enlarged.

"Oh, that's just too much," they complained. "We don't want to get carried away with all that excess—"

We are going to see excesses until Jesus returns for His bride, until the perfect is revealed. There will always be some people who will dance before the Lord just because others are dancing, not because they're being led by the Spirit. There will be critics who say, "Well, I just saw a lot of flesh." I always tell them, "I'm delighted you did. It'd be pretty spooky if all you saw was a bunch of disembodied spirits."

For every counterfeit, there is something real. In some situations, there may be ten counterfeits to one genuine manifestation of the Spirit, but what that says to me is, "I've burst upon the real."

When I worked in a bank, I saw some counterfeit money that looked *so* real.

"I don't know how I'll ever be able to tell the difference," I said to the banker.

"Let me show you," he said. Then he took a real dollar bill and laid it alongside a phony one. I could tell the difference immediately.

"That's how you tell a counterfeit," the banker explained. "You put it alongside the real thing and look at it."

The same test will work in the spiritual realm. Instead of standing back and pointing our fingers at counterfeits, we should become the real thing and go stand alongside that which is only make-believe. That gets the counterfeit unveiled so the Lord can deal with the person deceived by it.

Some time ago, I was ministering in Canada. I had been there long enough to know the Canadians are generally more reserved than we are in the United States, and so I didn't expect the Holy Spirit to move in a very powerful way. But when I got up to minister, I had one of those double-portion anointings. And I didn't hold back; I just poured it out all over them. Those poor, proper Canadians were being exposed to an obvious outpouring of the Holy Spirit.

On the second night of the conference, at the altar call, I heard myself saying, "I want only Pentecostal people at this altar."

It scared me, and inwardly I cried out, "I do? God, you've gotta be kidding. I've never said such a thing in my life before now."

But He didn't pay any attention to my protests. He just had me continue, like a fearless lion.

"I don't know who you are," I said to the people, "and I don't know where you are, but God knows, and He's singled you out. We're going to sing a song, and while we sing, I want you to come up here."

The next thing I knew, there were about three hundred people up front, looking at me. I didn't know what to do next, because God hadn't told me yet, so I stalled for time, asking them to sing the song again.

While we sang, I was carrying on an inner conversation.

"God, what did you get them up here for?"

He didn't answer until we finished singing. Then it seemed that He said, "Open your mouth, Iverna."

I did, and this is what came out:

"You Pentecostals ought to stand ashamed in the presence of God tonight because with your background, you're finding fault with the charismatic people in your community. Some of you need to make things right, and I'm going to give you the opportunity—right now."

Well, God broke through, and heaven broke out. I watched mothers and daughters hugging one another, making things right, people running from the front to the back and from the back to the front of the sanctuary—Pentecostals and charismatics crying and hugging and blessing one another. Coasts were being enlarged all over the place.

When it was over, the Lord let me preach.

The next morning, a little lady walked up to me and said, "I was one of those who came forward last night. I'm the wife of a Pentecostal preacher, and I have been hard on the charismatics. Worse than that, I have refused to recognize the charismatic renewal as a move of God. I did not know it was until after that altar call. Now that God has turned me around, I'd like for you to pray that when I go home, I can somehow impart the revelation of truth that God is doing a new thing."

I praised the Lord that she would no longer have to stand back and resist and weigh and contemplate and worry and wonder, but that she was ready to let God enlarge her coast.

Sometimes the Lord begins to enlarge our coasts by pulling back the rug of success. In recent months, ministers and pastors all over the country have been telling me, "We're frustrated. Things we used to do just don't work any longer. Advertising, special programs, yard sales, and attendance contests aren't bringing people in the way they did once."

Instead of sympathizing, I've learned to say, "Hallelujah!"

The look in their eyes says, "Hey! What's the matter with you? I've always suspected you were a little bit crazy, but—"

"That tells me God has His hand on your life," I tell them. "He has a divine plan to increase you, to enlarge you, and in order to do that, He must let the old things pass away. He fixes it deliberately so the old methods *can't* work any more. Nothing less than the flow of His life through you is going to satisfy Him *or* His people."

If there was ever a day in which the church needed to make Jabez' prayer, "Enlarge my coast," personal, it's today. We've been so limited in the past by our old teachings, our preconceived ideas, and our prejudices that we've been afraid to trust the Spirit of God to move.

"It's okay with me if other people want to clap their hands or hold their arms up in the air or get all excited about the Lord, but it's just not for me," I've heard folks say. They've limited their concepts of the workings of God to the things they have known in the past. They have been unwilling to receive the power of God for their own lives and churches.

God and I

Jesus said, "Blessed [in an enviable position, a happy state] are they which do hunger and thirst after righteousness: for they shall be filled" (Matt. 5:6). The Greek word for filled means "gorged."

Some people go to meetings hungry, starved for the things of God. He feeds them, and they are truly blessed. Others sit with no hunger at all, feeling guilty about it. Jabez' prayer, "Enlarge my coast," is a good one for them. They could add to it a confession of where they find themselves.

"O God, I'm so satisfied with what I have. I'm so content with where I am that I haven't been seeking more of you. I confess that as sin in me and ask you now to enlarge my coast. Increase in me an awareness of who you are. Make me able to behold you high and lifted up, with your own holy presence filling the temple. Enlarge my coast any way you want, so I can contain more of you. Work in my life until I have the very heart of God toward your people."

When we begin to pray that way, we begin to grow toward spiritual maturity.

The life of Abraham as it is recorded for us in the Old Testament is a picture of a man whose coasts were greatly enlarged:

> Now the Lord had said unto Abram, Get thee out of thy country, and from thy kindred, and from thy father's house, unto a land that I will shew thee: And I will make of thee a great nation, and I will bless thee, and make thy name great; and thou shalt be a blessing: And I will bless them that bless thee, and curse him that curseth thee: and in thee shall all families of the earth be blessed. (Gen. 12:1-3)

All Abraham had to do to receive God's blessing of having his territory vastly enlarged was to leave his country, his kindred, his father's house, everything he had known, everything which represented security and success.

"But where shall I go, Lord?" Abraham might have asked.

"I will show you as you start moving out," God might have told him.

"That's a tremendous sacrifice you're asking me to make, Lord," Abraham could have protested, "to leave my home and walk and walk and walk, not knowing where I'm going. What will I get for my trouble?"

"I will bless you," the Lord promised. "I will greatly enlarge your coast."

Somehow, that was enough for Abraham, and he came out of his familiar surroundings and began to walk in the Lord.

Most Christians find it difficult to walk in the Lord. Walking involves growing, **and** how we resist it! We'd far rather settle down on a comfortable plateau somewhere. And when the Holy Spirit has finally worked in us to overcome our resistance and enlarge our territory by helping us walk to a new level of faith, we say, "Whew! I'm glad that's over. It was a real struggle. Now I can rest for a while. Hallelujah!"

But that's not what the Lord has in mind.

"What are you doing?" He asks us.

"Why, I'm standing firm, Lord," we tell Him, delighted at our progress, basking in the pleasure of our newly enlarged territory.

"But I had in mind that you'd keep on walking," He tells us.

Abraham continued to walk, and whenever he came to a place where there was no water, he dug a well.

We don't do that. We're likely to arrive at a new place and head for the latest newspaper, looking for wells already dug by somebody else. We check to see if there's a Full Gospel group, a Spirit-filled church, a prayer group that's charismatic. . . .

But God is trying to teach us to dig new wells today. That's why He's put us where we find ourselves (Acts 17:26-27, TEV).

God and I

"Here's a shovel," He tells us. "Start digging."

God has told us in His Word that His Holy Spirit will be in us a *well* and out of us a *river* of living water (John 7:37-39). The well is of benefit to us, but we have to uncap it and let it flow before God can use it to bless other people. As we begin to praise the Lord, His presence flows out to magnify His name.

It seems as if sometimes the Lord plucks us out of a comfortably green oasis, where everything is fine, and sets us down in a parched desert in the midst of a thirsty people. They're in worse shape than we are, because they have no wells. The well inside us can satisfy everyone's thirst when we let it produce the flow of life that is Jesus.

"Hey, you guys, where's the well?" we might holler upon our arrival at the dry-looking place.

"Listen, man," they tell us. "We've been about to die of thirst ourselves. There's no well around here for miles. But we've been praying that God would show us some water. Frankly, we're about to give up because we haven't seen any evidence of life—"

"Oh, don't give up," we cry suddenly. "There is a river—"

As we begin to minister to them with the Word of God, our well becomes active again. And out of our innermost being flow streams of life-giving water. Blessings come, our territory is further enlarged. And a new oasis is formed.

When Christians get together to praise the Lord, they stir up the faith that is in them, and they are able to go forth with their shovels, believing God that through their ministries, blessing can be channeled to all who are thirsty. The water that is in them becomes clearer and clearer, blessing more and more abundantly.

A long time ago, Pentecostals dug some wells. Then the charismatics came along and dug some new ones. But the wells of the Pentecostals were clogged with exclusiveness and legalism, and the wells the charismatics dug were rather shallow. God let it happen so that no one could get too puffed up.

When none of us were exactly content with what God had accomplished through us, we decided to get together and try to figure it out.

"Great!" The Lord gave our coming together His full endorsement from the beginning. As a matter of fact, it was His idea.

"Here's my shovel," He said, offering us His written Word and His Word made flesh as tools to examine the wells that weren't producing as they should. "If you'll use prayer and praise along with real study of my written Word and real abiding in my Word made flesh, and start to dig, you'll begin to see such a flow of living water as will amaze you. There'll be springs of living water in every valley; there'll be streams of living water through the driest deserts; the coast of your productivity for me will be enlarged beyond measure."

But that was never the end of it. God didn't let us rest in our newly formed oasis or on our laurels; He told us to keep on walking, to keep on spreading the blessing as He commanded us in the Great Commission.

Some of us think we have earned a right to say to God, "But Lord, I have already walked so far. I came out of the narrow place where you found me. Remember what I used to be? Why do you keep at me to keep going? I'm already out of that place into a much bigger territory."

"So you are," He agrees. "So you are. You're out of that place, but you're not yet in the place to which I have called you, the promised land where you can rest."

Abraham had to keep walking until he got to the place where the Lord wanted him, and we have to keep walking too. It's as if the Lord says to us, "Yes, you've walked. But keep on walking, keep on appropriating, believing, accepting, hearing, doing, listening, being—"

Abraham didn't stop walking. And every time he came to a dried-up place, he dug a well.

But some of us are likely to dig a grave, because instead of being thirsty for what God can provide, we think it's the end of the line for us. I've left a lot of graves on my itinerary, but I've discovered that's not what God has in mind. I've finally learned to pick myself up and say, "God, I don't care how dry this place looks, I'm going to trust you for a supply of living water." And so I start digging in places that, in the past, I would have abandoned, heading down the dusty road, leaving a dry grave behind me.

The enlarging of our coasts is a continuing reality only when we are looking to God to supply the enlargement, even where it looks impossible.

God is calling all His people to dig wells of life in the most barren and hopeless-looking circumstances and situations. Where they are obedient to try it, Jesus fulfills His promise of giving them more than a drink, of giving them a well so that they and their fellow pilgrims might never thirst again. He is continually making His people a blessing, blessing them in the process, and enlarging the coast of His kingdom wherever they go.

Abraham kept walking, and he kept on digging. Finally, God said to Him, "Abraham, you're ninety-nine years old now. I wanted you to know what it was to cut yourself off from all earthly security and all claim that anyone had on you." Then He instituted the covenant of circumcision. The church is "the circumcision, which worship God in the spirit, and rejoice in Christ Jesus, and have no confidence in the flesh" (Phil. 3:3). Some of us have to renounce all confidence in the flesh more times a day than we can count.

"Lord, I know that unless you use me, I'm nothing," we say with our lips, while inside we may still be thinking, "I'm really pretty wonderful." But God sees our hearts and keeps snipping away at everything that isn't His will for us. With every snip, our coasts are enlarged.

And as we are obedient to unclog the well God has put within us, such a wealth of living water will spring up that there'll never again be famine for us. God could pluck us out of any situation, put us out in the desert, and say, "I want to add this to your territory, daughter. Cause this barren place to become fertile."

We could say, "All right, Lord," and set about to do it. We'd begin to see life and light growing there. People would come asking, "May I have a drink from your oasis?"

"Please do," we'd tell them. "There's plenty more where that came from. My coasts are being constantly enlarged."

6

"Thine Hand Be with Me"

After Jabez had prayed that God would bless him and enlarge his coast, he said, "God, that thine hand might be with me." The word for "hand" here is *yad*, signifying a hand with an open palm, a giving hand. As I understand it, when I pray for the hand of God to be upon me, I am asking Him to give me a number of things.

First, I am asking for power and authority. In the Old Testament, the king gave his signet ring to anyone who was authorized to speak for him, anyone who was entitled to use his power and authority. When they put the ring on, and pressed it into the wax on an official document, it meant, "The king himself has decreed thus and such a thing."

Jesus has given His followers authority like that. In essence, He said, "All power is mine, and I give it to you. Here's my signet ring. I'm placing it in your hand." In the Scripture, He said it like this:

> But ye shall receive power, after that the Holy Ghost
> has come upon you: ye shall be witnesses unto me.
> (Acts 1:8)

God and I

Because Jesus has given us His power and authority, when someone comes to us and says, "I have an awful need," we can pray for them with the authority God has given us:

"In the name of Jesus Christ, be it unto you as you have desired."

Christians often give more credence to the power and authority of Satan than they do to the authority of their Master. In charismatic circles, there's frequently more talk about the power of the enemy than there is about the power of God.

When Jesus came back from preaching down below to the Old Testament saints, He revealed himself to His disciples and said, "Look at my hands." I don't think He was pointing to the nail prints as much as He was saying, "Satan attempted to destroy my authority, but the Father has brought life and power back into my hands, and I present them to you, church." In other words, because the hand of God is with us, we have authority such as Jesus had.

When I was a child, we used to play a game. I don't remember the name of it, but it was like a tug of war.

"Whose side are you on?" we'd call out to one another.

"I'm on the Lord's side. Whose side are you?" they'd call back. Both sides would take hold of a long rope, all of us praying fervently that there would be more strength on the side of the Lord than on the side of the devil. There always was—and is today. He that is in us is greater than he that is in the world. We don't have to back down from anything when the hand of God is with us.

Many years ago, I attended a meeting in which an evangelist showed a film he had made during his travels around the world. It was a horrible movie, all about demon activity. After the showing, the preacher stood up and made an announcement.

"Church," he said, "I've had a vision. All over the United States of America, there are clouds of demons waiting to be released in the land. Within a period of no longer than ten years, I believe they're going to be set free over the major cities of America."

I was the main skeptic in the audience.

"Oh, brother," I groaned to myself. "This guy's traveled to Tibet and seen the demons like a mighty black cloud coming out of the mountains; he's traveled to Africa and been with witch doctors. Because of what he's seen as he's traveled all over, he's gone overboard. Now he thinks these things that happen in faraway places are headed for America. Poor guy!"

But he was right. The rest of us, who had been lulled into thinking the devil's activity would always be somewhere else, were the ones who needed to wake up. But before the release of these demons, there was a grand outpouring of God's Holy Spirit to equip us to deal with them. I'm not referring to exorcism, though that is the privilege of the believer to use when it is necessary, but about the awareness of the protection God has given the believer. The Holy Spirit has caused an increasing knowledge of the power of God within us.

"Beloved, now are we the sons of God" (1 John 3:2), we read, and as we have come to experience that reality, walls have been broken down, and Christians, under the powerful presence of the Holy Spirit, have sought one another out for fellowship and shared their testimonies of God's deliverance and protection.

Along with the outpouring of the Holy Spirit, there have been teachers coming forth all over the world—in New Zealand, America, Australia, Africa, Arabia—great men of God with a burden to teach the Word. Pastors who had been known only in a small territory resigned their pastorates and began to travel everywhere, ministering to the body of Christ.

When their teaching had had time to find a firm rooting place in those who walked not in the counsel of the ungodly, God was able to plant them as trees of living water (Ps. 1). Only then did He say to the demons, "All right. You can do your thing. But leave my people alone."

And the demons began to do their thing, but they were not permitted to touch God's people, and so they didn't.

"Touch not mine anointed" (1 Chron. 16:22) doesn't mean, "Don't talk about your pastor." It is God's warning to the ungodly: "You dare not touch any of my people, because if you do, you're going to have trouble." All through the Old Testament, God warned that His people were the apple of His eye, and the world was not to trouble them. "I will bless those who bless my people," He said. "Furthermore, I will curse those who curse my people" (Gen. 12:3, paraphrased).

When Balaam was called upon by Balak to curse the people of the Lord, he couldn't do it. What came out of his mouth was, "Blessed be the people of the Lord."

"Wait a minute, buddy," Balak challenged him. "That's not what we're paying you to say. Take another view of the scene."

Balaam looked again, a second and third time, and said, "Man, all I can see is the way those people are encamped—reminds me of a cross. Blessed be the people of the Lord!" By way of apology he explained, "God has blessed, and I cannot reverse it. God is not a man that He should lie or change His mind" (Num. 23:19, paraphrased).

Christians today are encamped as the Israelites were encamped, protected by the cross, the protection of the hand of God.

I'm not a demon-chaser unless one happens to stick his ugly head up where I happen to be. Then I don't believe in backing down from them.

A few months ago, I was ministering in a church in the East. Elders were with me to meet the needs of the prayer line that had come forward. A young man approached me with a sickening, sensual look.

"I want you to pray for me," he said. "I can't look at a woman without desiring her."

I recognized the enemy at a glance.

"Are you really ready to be set free from this?" I asked him.

"Oh, yes," he replied, obviously enjoying every minute of the attention.

I stepped back and said, "In Jesus' name—"

That's all there was to it. The demon left, and the man fainted. (Most of the elders looked as if they were going to join him.)

We don't have to call in demon specialists to handle these things. Jesus has given this power, this authority, to every Christian who will have it. I'm not talking about fraudulent Christians. If you're playing games, you'd better stay away from demons. But God's people, those who have been filled with His Spirit, those who have had the blood of Jesus applied to their lives, can be totally fearless in the face of every foe. In fact, according to my understanding of the Word of God, the devil ought to run from us without our saying a word.

The young man eventually got up from the floor, and a few weeks later I had a letter from one of the elders saying that he had received the fulness of the Holy Spirit and was moving on with God.

When the hand of God is upon us, we have the power to make that kind of a difference in human lives.

Second, when I pray for the hand of God to be with me, I'm asking for His protection. The Psalmist said, "His right hand, and his holy arm, hath gotten him the victory" (Ps. 98:1).

What kind of victory? All kinds. To begin with, victory over every kind of fear.

Listen to the conversation around you. People are saying, "Oh, I'm afraid I'm catching cold."

"I'm afraid I'll miss something."

"I'm afraid I'll get into error."

"I'm afraid I'll go off the deep end."

"I'm afraid—"

God and I

God does not want us to be fearful. He doesn't give us a spirit of fear, but one "of power, and of love, and of a sound mind" (2 Tim. 1:7). That means that instead of succumbing to fear, we can stand with firm confidence in what we know of God's love for us.

A young woman came to me for prayer one day because she was afraid. She was contemplating a major move in her life, and the insecurity of the unknown had let the enemy move in ahead of her.

Before I prayed for her, I had to ask a few questions.

"You've already burned your bridges behind you, so you can't go back to where you were, but if God reveals to you between now and the time you are to leave for your new work that you *shouldn't* go, are you willing not to go?"

"Yes."

"If you don't feel that God is stopping you, and you go ahead to this new venture and everything falls apart, are you willing to say, 'I blew it'?"

"Yes."

Then I took her hand and said, "In Jesus' name, I command the spirit of fear to be gone from you." And it was gone, just like that. Believers can avail themselves of victory over fear if they are really submitted to His will, if they have invited God's hand to be upon them.

Fear is one of the major factors in psychosomatic illnesses; God never intended for fear to be a part of His church. We don't have to be afraid of anything, because He protects us. We don't even have to be afraid of making mistakes.

When my brother Judson and I were pastoring a church together, we led people down blind alleys more than once. We'd see something some other church was doing that looked good. And we'd take our whole congregation and head in the same direction the other church was going. Before long we'd be aware we were in a blind alley, approaching a dead end. When we'd cry to the Lord about it, we'd hear, "That isn't what I told you to do. That's what I told that other church to do. It isn't for you."

"Sorry, Lord," we'd say. We'd apologize to the people too and tell them, "Church, turn back around. We need to get back out of this blind alley."

What did the people do? They turned around. There was no harm done; we'd all learned something. The protection of the Lord is there to correct us, to turn us back around when we have headed in a wrong way.

Looking back at some of the things in my own life, I'm amazed at the literal protection of the Lord. I did some of the most ridiculous and dangerous things when I was young. But the protection of the hand of the Lord was there, with victory over dangers I didn't even see. He had sent His holy angels to keep watch round about me, and I kept them busy.

I tell people my angel's resigning. Can't you hear him? "I had Iverna all last year. It's time for somebody else to take over."

Not only does the hand of the Lord give us power and afford us physical protection, He protects us spiritually as well.

No child of God should fear he might become demon possessed unless he's inviting demons to move in by his involvement with Ouija boards, witchcraft, mind control, astrology, and other things forbidden in God's Word. If we're doing those things, we're inviting trouble and we're entitled to it. But if we're serving the Lord, reading His Word and being obedient to it, then we're covered by the blood of Jesus and we're walking in that divine protection.

These are days of such rebellion, terror, anarchy, demon activity, and filthiness that we need the protection of God's hand more than ever before. There's no victory for us without it. A lot of people are in despair over the condition of the world. They look around and see that we're unsound financially, we're unsound scientifically, we're unsound politically, we're unsound philosophically, and social work isn't working any more. . . .

When people see us smiling, they may ask, "What's the matter with you? Don't you know about the problems?"

"Sure," we can tell them. "We know about the problems, all right, but we know an answer that's bigger than the problems. Hallelujah!" In giving the reason for the hope that is in us (1 Pet. 3:15), we present Jesus.

This *is* the day the Lord has made. We *can* rejoice and be glad in it. In one way of looking at things, we've never had it so good. The gray days are over, the days when we had to question what was right and wrong for us as Christians in the world. People aren't concerned any longer about the minutiae that used to take up our time, whether or not it was right to go here, to go there, to wear this, to wear that. The Lord had said that in the last days the filthy was going to become more filthy and the holy was going to become more holy (Rev. 22:11), and already it has happened to such a remarkable degree that the least discerning among us can know what is good and what is bad.

Five years ago, I would drive along the street and cluck at the obscene titles on the movie marquees of adult theaters. Today, the same movies are on television. But in the face of deteriorating standards all around, the church can still walk with heads up as children of the most high God.

In days gone by, many Christians walked around with their heads hanging low, their eyes downcast, because they knew they were professing one thing and living another. They talked victory, but they lived defeated lives. They talked healing, but they were sick in every way.

It's different today. It's as if the Lord has said, "All right, people. You've suffered defeated lives long enough because of your unbelief. I will begin again to show signs and wonders following the preaching of my Word—if you will rise in faith and dare to believe." This is what restoration is all about.

Another way in which the hand of God is upon us for our protection is written in Psalm 32:

> For day and night thy hand was heavy upon me: my moisture is turned into the drought of summer. (Ps. 32:4)

The same thought is echoed in the New Testament: "Humble yourselves therefore under the mighty hand of God, that he may exalt you in due time" (1 Pet. 5:6).

The heavy, chastening hand of God and the mighty, humbling hand of God spoken about in these verses is one of the greatest protections offered to the body of Christ.

If I did not believe in the chastening hand of God, I would be afraid to teach or preach, for fear I might say something that was not of God. But I know He is able to correct me before I have ventured far off the right path; He has done it many times. Sometimes He has pointed out a particular Scripture and asked me to read it to Him:

> Trust in the Lord with all thine heart; and lean not unto thine own understanding. (Prov. 3:5)

"What did you do today that was out of my will for you, Iverna?" He's asked me.

"I leaned on my own understanding, Lord. But now that you've brought it to my recollection, I'm sorry, Lord. I'll go before the people and straighten things out."

He's let me do that.

There are not many female traveling ministers today. I'm not invited to fellowship with the traveling men ministers. That makes it a lonely road sometimes. I'm not talking about the times when I feel I need somebody to talk to, but the times when I wonder, "God, what if I get off? What if my doctrine takes a little curve? What's to prevent my leading a whole bunch of people into error, Lord? Will there be someone to correct me?"

That awareness made me pray, "Lord, let Thy hand be upon me to chasten me when I err. Call me back when I begin to stray. I don't want to be able to manipulate you; I don't want to be successful at having my own way; I want your way for my life. Chasten me, Lord. Keep me on the right path."

I know He's the only one I can really trust; He's the only one with no axes to grind. His total interest in me is to make me like His Son. I can trust Him to keep me straight.

"Yes, purge me, Lord," I invite Him. "Cleanse me, purify me, transform by your grace whatever is necessary when I speak too much, when I don't speak enough, when I sound too harsh—"

I began to pray that prayer a number of years ago, and from that time until now, the Holy Spirit has kept tabs on my ministry. Sometimes He has pointed out, "Iverna, you need to apologize for saying that."

He corrected me one day when I was standing before an audience of over two thousand people. I didn't exactly like it, but I had to stand before them and say, "I have hurt some of you by a wrong statement I made, and I want to ask you to forgive me."

A man fell from a cliff one day, and as he was falling, he reached out and grabbed hold of a limb. He held on for hours and hours until his hands were so weak he couldn't hold on any longer. Then he released his hold, thinking he would plunge to his destruction on the rocks many feet below. Much to his surprise, he fell only three feet—to perfect safety!

Many of us have spent half a lifetime hanging on for dear life.

When anyone mentions Calvary to us, or says, "You've got to go to the cross," we get scared and hang on all the harder.

"I don't want to talk about the crucified life," we protest. "I believe in *living*, not *dying*."

The Lord lets us hang on as long as we can stand it. When we finally give up and let go, surrendering all we are and all we have to Him, it's as if we let go and fall three feet to safety. There's a humbling moment of relinquishment in which we say, "Father, into thy hands I commit my spirit. I give up all claim on my life, my possessions, my will, and my mind. You take them and do what you will with them. I give up. You are Lord."

At that point, we are ready to enter into real kingdom living.

As I travel from place to place, I have plenty of opportunity to hear about the things that keep people from committing their spirits into the hands of the Lord: cigarettes, a girl a man wants to marry, a man a girl mants to marry, a job, twenty-five years' seniority, a house, some silly little thing that has become a mountain to them.

"Oh, but I can't give this up," they say. "And God has told me that if I'm to surrender my spirit into His hands, I'll have to let go of it."

Listening to them, I have to say, "I wish I didn't understand you, but unfortunately, I do. I know what it is to hold on to the most preposterously small, insignificant thing in life and say, 'But I want this, I want it, I want it. I can't let it go.' But the Lord didn't leave me in that agony forever, and after a long period of time, my knuckles white and aching, I let go, maybe almost in disgust, saying, 'All right then, have it your way.' The moment I did that, the blessing of the Lord began to so flood my entire being that I forgot all about the thing I thought I couldn't live without. I found that my total security and all my joy and peace were in having His hand upon me, and not in having my own way at all."

God and I

The security we have in His hand was expressed by Jesus when He declared, "You are mine. You are right here in the hollow of my hand, and no man shall be able to pluck you out of it" (John 10:28-29, paraphrased). That's especially good news for us in a day when so many Christians are going around with big erasers, trying to wipe names out of the Lamb's Book of Life.

Just as there is power and authority in the hand of God, and protection and security in the hand of God, so there is provision in the hand of God. We read, "When thou openest thine hand, they are filled with good things" (Ps. 104:28, KJV, TAB).

I asked my brother, "How's business?"

"Wonderful! God has just given me a Christian business manager. Things are going real smooth."

That says to me that God has His hand on that life. When God puts His hand on a life, it's there for provision as well as for power and protection. God provides for us.

Some of us cheat ourselves out of His provision by insisting on having our own way.

"Lord," we say to Him, "here are my plans. Bless them, for Jesus' sake."

He looks them over and says, "Sorry. But I don't like your plans. They don't represent what I had in mind for you. Tell you what I'll do. Have a look at this set of plans—"

We look them over.

"Naw, I don't like them."

"What are we going to do?" the Lord asks us then. "You don't like my plans; I don't like yours."

"Guess it's a stalemate," we acknowledge.

"That's fine with me," the Lord tells us. "You go your way, I'll go mine."

Off we go, thinking we can bring our own plans to fruition without His help.

I did that once. I left the ministry and went back into selling.

I'd always been able to sell before I went into the ministry. Now, I should be sharper than ever at it, I thought. Besides, I had a great product, and there were lots of people out there who needed it.

"I don't need the Lord to help me sell," I told myself. "Just give me a product, a price, a person, and the deal will be closed."

Guess what. I was a total flop. I was so unbelievably unsuccessful, the company sent a manager from Portland to sit in with me on a presentation to see what was going wrong. He was more baffled than ever after watching me at work.

"I have never in my life seen a demonstration of this merchandise given more convincingly," he told his supervisor. "I felt like buying the merchandise myself, all of it. It was the craziest thing. I watched the prospective customers, and I could tell they were sold on it; they were ready to open their pocketbooks and sign on the dotted line. Mrs. Tompkins quit at exactly the right moment—but the whole thing froze."

As he stood there shaking his head, I stood there, too, and heard a word from the Lord. "It'll stay frozen, too, Iverna. The anointing I gave you to 'sell' the gospel of peace must never be used for another purpose."

I was convinced.

"Lord, show me those other plans again, will you?"

He did, and this time, I thought they looked great.

God gives us His provision, but only when we are letting Him be Lord of how He provides.

The guidance of the Lord is another thing that comes when His hand is upon us. The Psalmist said, "If I take the wings of the morning . . . even there shall thy hand lead me, and thy right hand shall hold me" (Ps. 139:9-10).

We are being guided by the Lord, even when His leading is through "life's tempestuous sea." If He always led us through flower-strewn pathways, we'd be totally unprepared to minister to anyone whose life was over a rocky course of highs and lows, ups and downs, ins and outs. When we have asked Him to make us a blessing, there will be consequences.

"Come this way, my child," He might say to us. "There are many who need to learn the things I will teach you along this path. But we will walk it together, you and I. Other people may not understand why you're taking this path, but you and I will know that I led you here to get glory for myself."

Many Christians condemn themselves for being on what seems to be the wrong path.

"Somewhere back there, I should have done something different," they wail. "But it's too late now."

We all need to realize we're exactly where we ought to be if our hearts are open to God to know His will. He *is* leading us. The Word tells us this in many Scriptures:

> The meek [the teachable ones] will he guide in judgment: and the meek will he teach his way. (Ps. 25:9)
> Teach me thy way, O Lord, and lead me in a plain path, because of mine enemies. (Ps. 27:11)
> Teach me to do thy will; for thou art my God: thy Spirit is good; lead me into the land of uprightness. (Ps. 143:10)
> The Lord shall guide thee continually, and satisfy thy soul in drought. (Isa. 58:11)

In seeking guidance from God, the first thing we need to look at is our attitude. Do we want the purposes and intentions of God to be carried out in our life? If our answer to that is yes, our next prayer can be, "Lord, I am seeking you first, and I'm asking you to give me the desires of my heart. If what I'm wanting is something you don't want me to have, then I ask you to change my desires to make them line up with your will."

Having prayed that, I go ahead and make plans, subject to His leading me to change them. "You can't steer a ship that's not in motion" seems to apply here.

I've heard some teach that we should do nothing until we have a definite word and confirmation of that word. It seems to me that one result of such teaching is to call everything to a halt while people wait for handwriting on the wall or something fantastic happening in the sky. But when God said we were to have the mind of Christ in us, He wasn't saying we shouldn't think. He was saying we should. God can use our human minds when they are renewed to be God-directed and Christ-centered.

As I make plans, I say, "Lord, these are subject to your approval. If I'm headed in the wrong direction, close doors or change my mind. I will repent." And then I go ahead. It seems to me that God gives us a lot of room for personal choice in some matters. When we pray to know His will, it's as if He says, "What do you want to do, kid?" If all we can do in reply is to stammer, "I-I-I d-d-don't know," He'd be justified in asking, "If you don't know what you want to do, why should I?"

Often we fail to receive guidance from the Lord because we are not teachable. If He can't instruct us in the way, He won't lead us in it. Teachableness is a prerequisite to receiving guidance.

I've had people come to me and ask to receive the Baptism in the Holy Spirit. I talk to them about it, learn that they have some understanding of who the Holy Spirit is, and the consequences of His coming into a life. I make sure they know the Scriptures promising that He is given to those who ask, and I show them that in New Testament times, the Holy Spirit was something imparted by the laying on of hands. When we have gone through all that, I lay my hands on them—but they don't receive the Holy Spirit.

"Lord, you promised that if anybody would ask, he'd receive," I've complained. "What's wrong? These people have asked, but—"

Going to their pastors, I've inquired about some of these people. I don't have to do that any longer, because I know what the answer will be. In every case, the person who failed to receive the Holy Spirit was someone who thought he had all the answers, a person who didn't want to learn, a person who wanted things his way or not at all.

God, in His mercy, could not bestow His Holy Spirit on such a person because He would not be able to instruct him in walking in the Spirit. Such persons continue to go their own way. The Psalmist said it like this:

What man is he that feareth the Lord? him shall he [God] teach in the way that he [the man] shall choose. (Ps. 25:12)

If you want to go with the Lord, and choose His way, He will set teachers about you to instruct you. You'll have all the guidance you'll need.

When some people have an important decision to make, they get ahold of God and ask Him to show them what to do. They're likely to pray with real agony, "God, hurry up and show me which way to go. I gotta know this week!"

That kind of prayer is probably better than nothing, but it's a baby prayer. We need to pray, "Lord, increase my understanding of your guidance." God wants us to know that He *is* leading us already. "The Lord *is* my shepherd. He leadeth me. Sometimes through suffering, sometimes through pain, but through whatever, He leadeth me."

What does the Lord want you to do today? He wants you to begin it by committing it to Him: " 'This is the day the Lord has made. I will rejoice and be glad in it' (Ps. 118:24). Make me a blessing to someone today, Lord. Make the words of my mouth and the meditations of my heart pleasing in your sight, O Lord, my strength and my redeemer." He wants us to stir up our faith daily, to the point where we can say in every situation, with the utmost confidence, "I *am* walking in the acceptable, good and perfect will of God."

Some of us have read so many books about how to find the will of God that we are confused by all the advice. We find it hard to know whether we're in His will or not. And yet the Scripture says, "Rejoice evermore. Pray without ceasing. In every thing give thanks: for *this is the will of God in Christ Jesus concerning you*" (1 Thess. 5:16-18, italics mine).

We're in His will when we're doing those things that He has commanded.

Any Christian who is not in the will of God is aware of the fact. When I was out in the world backsliding, nobody ever had to come up to me and tell me, "Iverna, you're out of the will of God." I knew it. In the same way, God doesn't have to come to the church and say, "You're in my will; I'm proud of you, son (or daughter), and glad you're doing a good job." He expects us to *expect* Him to lead, and we are to follow.

Whenever someone comes to me and says, "Iverna, please pray I'll find the will of the Lord for my life," I always tell them, "You're in His will already."

"How do you know?" they ask next.

"Simple," I explain. "Because you want to be in His will, you're in it. The only persons who are outside the will of God are those who are in rebellion against Him. If you're not in rebellion, if you want to be in His will, you're in it."

"But—but—" people sputter sometimes, "are you *sure*?"

"Look," I tell them, pointing to John 7:17, "if God isn't great enough to show you His will for you when you've made it plain you want to be in it, He isn't a big enough God to serve."

The enemy has a whole bagful of tricks to deprive us of this certainty. He'll come along and whisper in your ear, "Better watch out. You're probably not in God's will. You better slow down and go apart somewhere and seek His face."

If you listen to the enemy and withdraw from the action, you'll quit praying for people, you'll quit participating in the processes of God that are designed to mature you, and Satan will have you stagnating on the sidelines instead of going forward doing the will of God. You may waste five years seeking the will of God, when if you knew who you were in Him, you'd realize you were in His will already.

Some people have the erroneous notion that the Lord has to give them specific directions for each little thing they do. But I've found there is a wide latitude in the will of God for our lives. One illustration comes from the life of my brother Judson.

Jud loves music, and one day he sat down in a "music chair." It was a weird-looking thing to me, plastic, wired for sound, with speakers pointed at him from all directions. It had been marked down from around four hundred dollars to about two hundred in a special sale, and Judson had a real yearning in his heart for that particular piece of furniture. But he had grown up in a parsonage where he felt luxuries were not meant for him. He had turned his back on the chair, but he kept thinking about it so much that he prayed, "Lord, please show me whether or not I can have that chair."

Two or three days passed after he had prayed, and he was on a plane going somewhere. No one was in the seat beside him, and Judson was just talking to the Lord, and listening to the Lord talk to him.

"About that chair, Lord," Judson said at one point in the conversation. "You know I'd really like to have it, but—"

"Son, if you want that chair, quit stewing about it and go ahead and buy it. Personally, I don't care whether you have the chair or not. But you seem to have your heart set on it, and I like to give my children the desires of their hearts so—"

Judson now owns the fantastic musical chair. He enjoys it, and the Lord doesn't seem to mind at all.

Some teachers say we should never ask for anything for ourselves unless there is a spiritual purpose behind our asking. I can't agree with them. It *is* wrong to ask for things that I might be glorified, that I might spend the gifts on the lusts of my heart, that I might have the satisfaction of hearing people say, "Oh, what a great woman of God!" That's forbidden self-indulgence, but it *is* all right for me to ask for some things I don't need, things that I simply want.

Before God is anything else to us, He is our heavenly Father, and even earthly fathers are thrilled to give their children the desires of their hearts. Three months before Christmas, the children start to say, "Dad, I'd love to have—" And dad starts planning to get the things for them if it's at all possible.

When we first come to the Lord, we have a tendency to ask Him about every tiny little thing.

"Lord, is it okay if I do the dishes now? Lord, have I spent enough time in prayer? Lord, shall I go to work today?"

In the beginning, babies have to be led every step of the way, and the standard has to be taught over and over again. But after a while, when we have learned the standards, we learn we don't have to ask so many questions.

Suppose, for instance, that I'm thinking of buying a new car. I go to the Lord and ask Him about it.

"I need a word from you, Lord. Should I buy the new car—or not?"

"Iverna, the only word you need from me is a question: Can you afford to make the payments?"

If my answer is no, I don't need a word from the Lord. A word from my banker will do.

"It's time for my people to come to an understanding of how I deal with them," God seems to be saying to the church today. He's dispelling ignorance on the part of His people with a veritable flood of teaching in books, on tapes, and at conferences such as we've never had before. He's not waiting on our ignorance the way He seemed to do in the past. It's as if He is saying, "Let my people come to know what I do and what I say. Let them truly know that all things work together for good to them who love me and are the called according to my purpose. Let them know they can trust my hand to guide them."

Moses came to the point where he knew he could trust God for everything. When the Israelites came to the Red Sea and there seemed to be no way across, Moses said, "Lord, we don't have any boats. How are we going to make it across? Some of the people can't swim."

The Lord told him to hold up his rod, and Moses didn't argue with Him; he just did as he was told. The waters parted so the people could walk across on dry ground. Moses didn't question how God was going to do the thing; he just knew He was going to do it.

After Moses had been walking with the children of Israel for some years, he had seen many marvelous acts of God. He had learned, from experience, that God could do anything, that He could meet every situation, regardless of the need.

When the water was bitter, he said, "Lord, what can we do to sweeten the water?" The Lord told him to throw a certain tree in the water and it would be sweet. Moses followed the directions, and got the desired result (Exod. 15:23-25).

When the Israelites were thirsty and they had no water, Moses prayed, "Lord, they're thirsty again. And I don't see any water around here. What should I do this time?"

"See that rock over there?" the Lord said. "Smite it and water will come out."

It didn't sound likely, but Moses followed the directions, and again had his needs met (Exod. 17:3-6).

The New Testament tells us that everything that is recorded in the written Word of God is there for our instruction (2 Tim. 3:16). We're to learn from the things that happened to people in both the Old and New Testament times. In Moses' experience, we learn that no matter what the situation is, God knows the answer and will provide it if we ask Him. He's bringing us to the place in sonship where He can just breathe His will into us and we will do it.

One night I came in from a long meeting where there was so much ministry, I was utterly exhausted. Throwing myself across the bed in my hotel room, I complained, "Lord, I'm completely worn out. I know your Word is truth, and you say that your yoke is easy and your burden is light, but—"

"*My* yoke *is* easy," He reminded me.

"Well, please, could I get in your yoke then? The one I've been wearing isn't light at all. It's about to break my neck."

All this was going through my mind as I lay there in a state of exhaustion. He seemed to lift up a huge yoke and hold it above my head for a minute.

"All right," He said. "Just put your neck in there and I'll lead off. Wherever I go, you just follow along. You'll find this is the easiest yoke you've ever tried."

We started out together, and I said, "Oh, Lord, this is wonderful. I don't know why I didn't try this way sooner. No work, no load, I just follow along."

"I'm turning left at the next block," He said then.

"I'm not," I told Him. "I'm going to the right."

"You're asking for a broken neck then," He said, ever so gently, and I saw the secret. When you're yoked with Him, you go His way, or you wind up in traction somewhere with your head about broken off. That's how yokes work. I found out the hard way. I can show you my scars.

We cannot ask the Lord to show us His way and then

continue to go our own way unless we want to get our necks broken.

When Jesus was about to leave this world and return to the Father who sent Him, He lifted up His hands and blessed his disciples (Luke 24:50). In blessing them with His hands, He gave them power and authority, provision and security, protection and guidance, even the knowledge that they would be chastened when it was necessary. No wonder Jabez prayed, "that thine hand might be with me," and no wonder we are blessed when we pray for ourselves in the same way.

7

"Keep Me from Evil, that It May Not Grieve Me"

When Jabez had prayed that the Lord would bless him indeed, enlarge his coast, and keep His hand upon him, he also prayed that the Lord would keep him from evil, that it might not grieve him.

The word for grieve means, "to carve up, to cause worry, pain, or anger; to spoil by breaking in pieces." Jabez was saying, "God, if I do evil, if I get off your path, if I get away from your purpose for my life, I will hate myself. I will be broken to pieces, shattered. I will be filled with loathing and self-contempt. I'll be so angry with myself that I won't be useful to anybody. That's not what I want. That would grieve me, O Lord. Grant that this won't happen to me. Keep me from evil."

Most of the angers and resentments that cause us to walk in guilt and worry are the result of our sinning against ourselves. It's sometimes easy for us to forgive other people but so hard for us to forgive ourselves. Jabez seemed to know this, and he was saying, "God, I don't want to act in ways that will displease you and make me ashamed of myself."

Today the body of Christ is split into segments, carved into pieces with dissensions, divisions, and every kind of evil.

God and I

There's a cry in my spirit that says, "O Lord, I know you can't come until you have delivered us and kept us from evil that it might not carve us up into pieces and break us asunder. So deliver us that there can be a real unity among us, a real life-giving flow of the life of Christ."

All this can happen in the body of Christ as it happens in each one of us, as we become willing to reach for His ability to forgive one another and to receive His forgiveness for ourselves. A part of receiving that forgiveness for ourselves lies in extending it to others.

It is necessary for us to pray that God will keep us from breaking after we have asked Him to enlarge our hearts, because we will have the compassion of Jesus for suffering humanity. Human hearts cannot handle such compassion without cracking up.

My brother Judson was repeatedly laid on the shelf because of illness. I got on my knees before God for him one day, and I prayed, "Lord, I've seen this happen so often in Jud's life. Why, Lord? You've invested in him so much truth and insight and revelation; you've given him such understanding of your Word and such great ability to present it so the people can understand. Why does this sickness keep coming upon him to hinder him, Lord?"

The Lord showed me, and Judson himself came to understand, that the sickness came because his heart had grown so big. As he traveled throughout the world, he knew what it was to have men go out in front of his plane and try to keep it from taking off because they were so eager to have him remain and teach them a while longer. A heart that's been enlarged and tenderized by the presence of the indwelling Holy Spirit can't shoulder such a burden as that without breaking. Judson would be weeping as the plane took off, feeling such a responsibility for the people he was leaving behind that he could hardly bear it. But he had other commitments, a schedule to keep. And he had to learn that just as he was responsible for what God called him to do, so the Lord would complete the work He had allowed Judson to begin. That certainty was all that kept Jud from breaking to pieces and being rendered useless.

It doesn't bring glory to God when His people are broken to pieces by physical illness, nervous breakdowns, mental and spiritual distresses. Yet sometimes we have made such heroes and heroines of the people who minister to us that they've worked at a frenzied pace until they've fallen apart.

Someone gave me a little sign that said, "I'd rather burn out for the Lord than rust out." But I don't want to do either one of those things. I'd rather live, walking with Him and working with Him. Working *for* Him can wear you out, but working *with* Him is Life eternal.

One reason some of God's people are overworked today is that others are afraid to help share the load.

"Go and pray for so-and-so," I might tell a Christian. "She has a need."

"Oh, but I'm afraid I couldn't do it as well as you would," they hedge.

"Are you a child of the King or not?" I ask them.

When they nod meekly, I repeat the instruction.

"Okay, dear vessel, let Him meet the need through you. *Everybody* can be poured out to usefulness if they're willing."

There was a time when the evangelist was expected to bring the whole revival in his suitcase. He was expected to do everything. But today, there's much ministering of the people to one another. Little groups are huddling in the lobby, along the aisles, praying for one another. We are learning to claim the blessings and promises of God for one another.

Another kind of breaking can come about when we shoulder burdens the Lord never meant for us to bear.

When Isaac, the miracle son, was born, it must have been

the most exciting day of Abraham's life. But there were problems too.

Ishmael was always making fun. "Big deal. He's got the son you promised him now, God. But it's too late for him. I've ruled and reigned in this family for fifteen years, and there's no way Abraham can get rid of me. I'm his son too."

Sarah, being the instigator of the problem child, was grief-stricken. She came to Abraham complaining of the conflict and trouble that were resulting from the child Ishmael.

"Please send him away," she said.

"I can't," Abraham's sense of fairness said. "It wouldn't be right. God wouldn't want me to do a thing like that."

But God said, "Go ahead and send the child out, Abraham. He's not your burden. I'll take care of him." And Abraham did it.

One of the subtle problems that creeps into the lives of God's people even today is what I call false burdens. Some people will try to use you up, sap all your energy with their problems, and call on you interminably to minister to them. It's as if they were saying, "If you really love me, you'll let me usurp your life."

They'll have you on the phone the first thing in the morning, halfway through the day, and then they'll come and lean on your doorbell early in the afternoon so they can cry on your shoulder until the kids get home from school:

"I don't know what I'd do if I didn't have you. Nobody else cares about me."

When your husband comes home, starved for a decent home-cooked meal, he looks around in disbelief—beds not made, dirty dishes in the sink, laundry piled high, kids fussing because you haven't paid any attention to them, supper not even started. He doesn't say a word, but you can read his thoughts.

"What on earth has she been *doing* all day?"

"I've been working for the Lord," you tell him, but it doesn't sound convincing, even to you.

Either the Lord is Lord of your life, or He is not. And He is perfectly capable of being Lord of that other person too, if you'll wean her from reliance on you. I believe in love, in encouraging, in exhorting one another daily, but we need to hear from the Lord about these things. He can tell us how much time we are to spend with each one so that we're not drained of life before we have taken care of the needs of our families. When we do what we are supposed to do, there will be peace again in the house, just as there was when Abraham sent Ishmael and his mother away.

I know that mental breakdowns, ulcers, and many other ailments are occurring in the body of Christ today because the enemy is pressuring God's people, men and women with God's heart of compassion, and diverting their energies into burdens God never intended them to have. The enemy tries to get us overly concerned about things so he can break our health and lessen our faith.

People go to church without even enjoying it because they worry about all the things the people up front aren't doing according to *their* standard. This kind of thing used to get me. I went crazy, going from one place to another, hearing the second place sing choruses in a way different from how they were sung at the first place. And then one day, the Lord healed me of that kind of critical spirit.

We were singing, "It's a new day; it's a new revelation in a brand new way," and they were singing it all wrong. It grated on my nerves to the point that I was having a terrible time trying to keep from stopping them and saying, "Hey, wait a minute! Let me show you how you're supposed to sing that song."

After the service, some of us went out for hamburgs, as they call them in Canada. I was sitting beside a woman who had sung louder than anybody else in the congregation, obviously enjoying herself. Somebody brought up the subject of how much fun it was to sing all the new choruses that were making the rounds in the body of Christ. When they mentioned the one with which I'd been having such a bad time, I asked the woman next to me, "Have you been singing that chorus very long?"

My question sounded innocent enough, but I was just getting in gear to tell her how it ought to be sung.

"Quite a while—way before it ever came out in sheet music," she answered me. "You see, I'm the one who wrote it. Do you like it?"

I almost fell off my chair, but I learned something that night.

"Lord, thank you for that," I told Him under my breath. "From now on, I promise I'll just worship you. I won't care how they sing the songs."

Jabez' prayer that he might not be broken to pieces could be interpreted, "God, don't let me become useless."

Let's look at some of the things that could make God stop using us. In Ephesians 4:14-15 Paul mentions some of them:

> That we henceforth be no more children, tossed to and fro, and carried about with every wind of doctrine, by the sleight of men, and cunning craftiness, whereby they lie in wait to deceive; But speaking the truth in love, may grow up into him in all things, which is the head, even Christ.

Peter has this to say further:

> Ye therefore, beloved, seeing ye know these things before, beware lest ye also, being led away with the error of the wicked, fall from your own stedfastness. (2 Pet. 3:17)

Many things we blame on the enemy are really sins of the flesh, manifestations of our carnal nature. Most of us are our own worst enemies. The Lord has sent us to minister, and instead of ministering, we move out of the realm of faith to listen to all the garbage about what's wrong in the life of another. I'm learning to interrupt some of the excess verbiage, and just begin to pray, trusting God to reveal the *real* problem to me.

If I wait while someone tells a long, dragged-out problem to me, my own faith gets watered down with their faithless approach.

"I've tried this, and I've tried that, and I've tried everything," they'll tell me, "and it just doesn't work."

I don't need to hear all that.

"Do you want out, or not?" I ask them. "If you want out, God has a rope. He can throw it to you and reel you right in to the holy place if that's where you want to be. But it won't edify either of us to review all the details of the problem. Let's pray."

That's the way I can be useful, not by listening to all the garbage about what doesn't work.

We can often look at another person and read what's wrong with him simply by looking at his face. If we see despair on a person's face, it doesn't matter that we don't know any reason why she should be in despair—maybe we suppose she's happily married, the kids are doing well, and she's coping at the supermarket. But we shouldn't let our knowledge of the so-called facts make us useless in the situation. We can go right up to such a person and say, "I believe God wants to release the joy of the Lord in you. It'll bring new strength to your life." Most people will acknowledge they could use a little more strength, and when we say, "May I pray with you?" they'll receive our ministry with joy. We won't be useless, we'll be ministering life.

God and I

God's people have been hurt and beaten down with so much negative preaching that their faith levels are watered down to the point where they're afraid to believe God for anything. They're looking for someone who can minister life to them, and if I read my Bible correctly, we have the life of Jesus in us and can impart it to others.

Another application of the "keep me from evil so it might not hurt me" (1 Chron. 4:10, TAB) of Jabez' prayer has to do with the traits we have inherited from our parents or acquired from our course through life. Each of us has inherited a lot of things from our forebears. I blame my Cornwall heritage for my overly sensitive nature and unbelievable stubbornness. I used to defend myself for these undesirable familial traits by saying, "That's just the way I am. All Cornwalls are like that. Sure, I get my feelings hurt a lot, and sometimes I fly off the handle. But my mother was that way, my grandmother, her mother before her—we just can't help it."

But I've learned we can help it. We can break the curse that has been handed down from generation to generation by praying, "God, deliver me! Keep me from the evil that would break me. Deliver me from every tendency that does not glorify your name. Deliver me from my inheritance, from anything in the past that is second-best, from everything that would hinder my usefulness to you." He will hear the prayer and answer it in ways that will amaze us. We don't have to be victimized by our past; it has been redeemed. In Jesus, we can live in the now as if the past had never been.

I can look at Calvary and imagine Jesus saying to Satan, "All right, Satan. On August 22, 1929, in Reno, Nevada, a baby daughter is going to be born to Beulah and Espie Cornwall. They're going to name her Iverna, and she'll wind up doing a lot of things—she'll walk in rebellion and stubbornness, she will cheat and lie and marry and divorce and do a lot of other things that are not my best will for her. But I'm here right now to pay the penalty in advance for every wrong thing she's ever going to do. You can lay it all on me." On Calvary, when He said, "It is finished!" it *was* finished for all time.

I don't have to be trapped by my past; none of us do. Jesus has taken care of it all. When we can really believe that and appropriate it for our lives, we'll walk in a new way altogether, no longer rendered useless because of all the wrong things in our heritage and history.

In praying that God would keep him from evil, Jabez recognized that the past was a part of him, but he did not want to be limited by it.

"God, my name is Jabez. It means 'sorrowful.' Please keep me from being rendered useless because of my name. God, don't let me live up to my name. Let me live up to your power and strength, your joy."

As a teenager, I had a tendency toward depression. They called it "moodiness" in those days. When I was in a good mood, I was the life of the party. But God help us when I wasn't.

One day my daughter said to me, "Mom, I'm moody like you were, aren't I?"

"Yeah," I agreed. "You're a very moody person." She was moody in a different way. When she was in a good mood, she was a saint, but when she was in a bad mood, she wasn't a tyrant like me. She was still quiet and reserved, obviously a woman of God, but she would get so low that she could hardly smile at all for two or three days at a time.

"Well," Debbie wanted to know, "when you used to be moody, how did you get out of it?"

I didn't have to tell her. The moment she confessed she was interested in getting out, she was almost there. We went on to talk about these things a little.

"Debbie," I told her, "you don't have to be moody like I was. You don't have to take on any of the bad traits that were in my life. I don't have to be saddled with them either. Just look at me, decide what you don't like about me, and set out deliberately not to be like me in those areas. You'll make it because Jesus wants you to be perfect, in His image, not mine."

Unbelievers are stuck with whatever family they're born into, but believers are not. Our Lord meant it when He said, "Behold, I make all things new; I make believers into new creatures when they put their trust in me" Rev. 21:5 and 2 Cor. 5:17, paraphrased).

We can believe that because of Jabez' prayer, he became a man no longer sorrowful but full of the joy of the Lord.

There is nothing we'll ever need that is not provided for us in Jesus. Every fetter can be broken; every facet of our fallen inheritance can be redeemed; every sin of our life can be turned to His glory. But He won't do it while we're warring and fighting against Him with our wanting this, that, and the other thing. He won't violate our will. He works in us to *will* before He works in us to *do*.

The children of Israel had problems in this area. They continually said, "We want, we want, we want." One thing they wanted was quail. God said, "All right, you want 'em, you want 'em, you want 'em; you can have 'em and have 'em and have 'em."

It didn't take long for them to confess, "God, we're sick of what we wanted." The same thing happens to us, time after time, and eventually some of us learn that *our* wants are not the best for us.

If we don't want to be carved into bits, we have to become whole. We have to get it all together, to get heart and mouth to agree.

I was standing on a platform one evening, singing words of praise along with a congregation. My hands were in the air, and we were all singing about how we love Jesus. Suddenly I realized the words coming from me were a farce. I had a head knowledge of the fact that I loved Him because I knew He loved me, but there was no feeling of love in me. As I looked out at the congregation, I saw some people who were so obviously in love with Him, it showed in the gleam and sparkle of their eyes as they looked upward, singing their love to Him.

"Lord," I confessed, "I'm ashamed to tell you this, but I'm feeling carved up in little pieces. I'm all mixed up, Lord. I don't know what's wrong with me. My mind says I love you, but my feelings are void of any consciousness of your love toward me or mine toward you. What's wrong, Lord?"

"Iverna," He seemed to say, "your channel for giving and receiving love has been clogged because somebody hurt you. You've been afraid of being hurt again, so you've tried to protect yourself, saying, 'I don't want my heart to be broken any more, so I'll never love again.' That's why you can't love me right now. You're refusing to give in to love anyone."

I knew He had hit the nail on the head.

"That sounds right, Lord," I confessed. "But what can I do about it? I am fearful of making myself vulnerable and being hurt again."

His answer was straight from 1 John 4:10: "Herein is love, not that you love me, Iverna, but that I love you. It doesn't begin with you; it begins with me. Can you receive my love?"

"Oh, Lord, I can! I can do that. Lord, right now, I reach up and I receive your love for me." It was as if I got a whole armload of it and hugged it to myself. The channel was unclogged and I was really worshiping the Lord. I had entered the Holy of Holies, and I was in His presence. We were speaking words of love to one another. It was wonderful.

And it lasted. When I came down off the platform, I was shouting, "Hallelujah! I love you! Jesus loves you! Isn't Jesus wonderful?"

I counted the cost and realized it would be worth being hurt every day of my life not to be cut off from the sense of Jesus' love for me and mine for Him.

We can pray, "O God, keep me from evil, that it may not carve me up and make me afraid to be vulnerable to love. Keep me, Lord, from being shattered to pieces and rendered useless to you."

8

Answered Prayer

At the close of Jabez' prayer, we read, "And God granted him that which he requested" (1 Chron. 4:10). The word for "granted" here indicates that the granting was a progressive, continuing thing, an answer that continued to unfold over a period of time. God began to work, and kept on working in the life of the man who opened himself up to Him, saying, "Bless me, Lord, because without the blessing of the Lord, I'm rendered useless. Enlarge my coast, Lord. Break down the walls, the prejudices, the barriers and hindrances. Let God be increased and enlarged in me. Let my ministry be increased and enlarged without. O God, keep your hand upon me. Let me know your authority and your protection, your guidance and your provision and your chastening too. I've got to know that your hand is upon me, Lord. And keep my inheritance from impairing my usefulness to you. Keep me from being handicapped by the things other persons and circumstances have put into my life. Let me have the name and the nature of the Lordship of Jesus Christ so that I might be preserved in wholeness, united with the body of Christ."

As we pray the prayer that Jabez prayed for himself, a voice comes back from heaven: "I hear that prayer. And I, the Lord your God, am answering it."

A long time ago, we were taught that after we had prayed, we needed to wait years and years for an answer. We studied examples in the Word of God to teach us patience. Elisha, for instance, walked ten years with Elijah before he ever came into the ministry he desired. There are many other examples in the Scriptures in which time was a big factor in the fulfillment of the promises of God.

But in looking through God's Word, we also find a surprising number of persons who expected—and received—almost immediate answers to their prayers. Sometimes God answered before they called. Other times, the answer was so quick in coming, it must have been well on its way before the prophet ever placed his order.

God literally sent an apology to Daniel for the twenty-one-day delay between his prayer and the answer arriving on the scene. The angel Gabriel said, "Sorry about the delay, Daniel, old man. We had a little trouble getting through the problems upstairs—the prince of Persia tried to prevent your blessing, but Michael helped me handle it." The delay was brought about, not because God was unwilling to act speedily, but because Satan interjected a little interference.

Apparently David got a little better service:

In the day that I cried unto thee, thou heardest my prayer and answeredst me. (Ps. 138:3, paraphrased)

We don't usually teach that kind of immediacy today. We are more likely to teach people to wait on the Lord and not expect anything *too soon*. That is a mistake. Granted, there are times when we need to learn to wait on the Lord, but we should be in a state of expectancy every time we pray.

"Lord, move today," we should pray. Then, if we hear His

voice telling us to wait, we can say, "Amen." But there should be no more praying, "Lord, I just ask you to fill me with your love, your life, and your light, but there's no hurry. I don't mind waiting until next year. As a matter of fact, I'll be kind of relieved if I have to wait forever."

I think the Lord's answer to such prayers is, "Grant her petition—but put an indefinite hold on it." After all, if we're not interested in an immediate answer, why should He bother to send it special delivery? When we're not expecting an answer to our prayers, we're not exercising faith. We don't even expect God to do anything for us, and yet in all the accounts we read in God's Word, when people really prayed, God really moved. We're not to pray thinking maybe five years from now the Lord will answer our prayers. He wants to do it *now*.

Sometimes in intercessory prayer, God has to delay the answer until the person for whom we're praying has met the conditions necessary for receiving the answer. God doesn't violate their free moral agency, and it may take time for circumstances and events to bring things to a point where the person for whom we're praying will be able to receive what God wants to do for him. But when we're praying for ourselves and know that we have met the conditions, we can expect an immediate answer.

We can pray, "Lord, I want to know your will in this. Here is what I propose to do if it meets your approval. I've met your conditions: I've delighted myself in the Lord, and therefore I expect you to give me this desire of my heart or else root that desire out of me. Amen."

After such a prayer, we will experience one of two things. Either we will get the desire of our heart because God put the desire in our heart to begin with, or God will bring us to realize that's not what we really wanted after all.

I don't believe in *not* getting an answer to prayer. God can say no to my requests, but He can't ignore me if I fulfill my part of the conditions and if there are no barriers in me to prevent my receiving His answer.

If you've prayed a prayer and haven't received an answer, check yourself against the requirements on your part as laid down in Scripture. If you see you've met them all, you're entitled to go back before the Lord and say, "Now, God, you're a God who can't lie, and you promised to give, and I want to receive or know the reason why."

What are the requirements on our part? And what are some of the things that can keep our prayers from getting through to Him or His answers from getting through to us?

I see ten common barriers that prevent our receiving answers to our prayers. They are:

1) disobedience
2) secret sin
3) indifference
4) unmercifulness
5) instability

6) self-indulgence
7) unforgiveness
8) an unruly tongue
9) dishonesty
10) a husband-wife relationship that is out of order

Each of these factors is mentioned in the Scriptures, some with a number of case histories.

Disobedience. When we are openly disobedient to God, we can't expect a clear channel of communication to be open between us. "Now we know that God heareth not sinners: but if any man be a worshipper of God, and doeth his will, him he heareth" (John 9:31).

In the Old Testament, when the Israelites had been disobedient, God would not hear them (Deut. 1:45); and on several occasions, Saul cried out to the Lord but the Lord did not answer him (1 Sam. 14:37; 28:6).

If we're in rebellion against God about anything, we can't pray about another matter and expect to be heard. First, the area of our disobedience has to be cleared up. What can we say?

"God, I'm sorry. I repent right now. Please forgive me. I'll obey you."

Then we can get on with our prayers about other things.

Secret sin. Any secret sin in our lives blocks our communication with God. The Psalmist said, "If I regard iniquity in my heart, the Lord will not hear me" (Ps. 66:18).

Iniquity is secret sin, something in us that is hidden, a sin the world may not realize we have.

When we are living in open disobedience, we can't deny it. Everybody knows it. But we can keep secret sins pretty well hidden from people who pray for us. They might say, "God, I know this life is pure in your sight. She's given up everything to follow you, Lord."

All the time they're praising our virtuous uprightness, the Lord is saying to us, "Cheater, deceiver. You and I know about that thing down in the corner of your heart. Do you want to get it out now, do you want me to tell them about it, or shall we just not talk for a while? No answered prayers, for instance?"

Until we're ready to have the secret sin rooted out of us, we can't talk to Him and expect Him to hear.

Indifference. God tells us, "the effectual fervent prayer of a righteous man availeth much" (James 5:16). He doesn't tell us that indifferent prayers accomplish anything. If we're indifferent, we're not ready to receive an answer. In order to receive answers, we need to care enough to be specific, and to pray fervently, expecting an answer.

We need to decide what is really important to us and not to generalize, in order to prevent useless prayers that go like this: "Lord, if you want to bless me, that's fine with me. If you want to increase me, go right ahead. If you want to keep your hand on me, feel free. In fact, Lord—(yawn)—just figure out what you want to do and go ahead and do it. You have my permission. Whatever you want is okay with me."

Prayers of such an indifferent person won't move anthills, let alone mountains.

Unmercifulness. "Whoso stoppeth his ears at the cry of the poor, he also shall cry himself, but shall not be heard" (Prov. 21:13). This verse makes it pretty clear that if we ask for mercy but do not grant it, our prayers will be a waste of time and breath.

"Do you want mercy?" the Lord asks us.

"Lord, I sure do. I need a new batch of mercy every day."

"I give my mercy to the merciful," He says (Matt. 5:7). "If you won't be merciful to others, you can't ask for mercy for yourself."

When we put ourselves in a position that doesn't allow us to ask for mercy, we can't ask for anything else either, and our whole prayer life is wiped out.

Instability. The unstable man is guaranteed *not* to receive any answer to his prayers:

> But let him ask in faith, nothing wavering. For he that wavereth is like a wave of the sea driven with the wind and tossed. For let not that man think that he shall receive anything of the Lord. (James 1:6-7)

The wavering man isn't in a position to receive anything from the Lord because he doesn't know what he really wants. He's tossed to and fro, up and down. One day he wants God's will; the next day he wants his own will more.

"Bless me in this venture, Lord," he cries, fervently enough. The next day, he's abandoned that project already and dived into a new one. "Forget that other thing, Lord. Bless me in this one instead."

"Until you make up your mind about what it is you want me to bless, I can't help you much," the Lord says. "Besides that, my angel in charge of delivering answers to prayer can't ever catch up to your newest forwarding address."

Self-indulgence. Prayers that are prayed for wrong reasons, from purely selfish motives, are not answered. God's Word tells us:

> Ye ask, and receive not, because ye ask amiss, that ye may consume it upon your lusts. (James 4:3)

If we ask God for something in order to spend it on our own selfish desires, it wouldn't be good for us to have it, and He won't grant it, no matter how many times we ask Him.

"Lord, please grant me money and fame. Let my name be a household word. Let people everywhere fall all over themselves to get my autograph. I'd like to have a yacht, servants, jewels—"

Who prayed that prayer? A woman nobody ever heard of. She's somewhere standing in a soup line. God's answer to her self-indulgent prayer was an emphatic no.

Sometimes God has to withhold spiritual gifts because the individual who is asking isn't sufficiently mature to handle the consequences, but would use the result for his own gain.

Effective ministers of the gospel have the power of persuasion and the ability to create faith in their hearers, presenting their "product" in a way that makes people want what they are offering. These qualities are gifts from God.

Suppose a man is plentifully endowed with these gifts. He can walk into a situation where everybody is hopeless and in despair, listen to their woebegone tale of dismal circumstances and get them to rejoice in the certain knowledge that God is going to work everything out for such good, so fast, they can hardly wait. People have a natural tendency to put such a man high on a pedestal.

"When he prays, things really happen!" they say, and they're right.

Unless God has done a deep, heart-changing work in such a

man before investing him with such gifts, he's headed for trouble. The sign on his pedestal might read:

"Come one, come all. Let me pray for you. Only $4.98 per request."

Unforgiveness. It's good to pray for forgiveness, but here again, there are clear conditions to be met before God can forgive us in answer to our prayer:

> And when ye stand praying, forgive, if ye have aught against any; that your Father also which is in heaven may forgive you your trespasses. But if ye do not forgive, neither will your Father which is in heaven forgive your trespasses. (Mark 11:25-26)

In the Lord's prayer, we pray that God will forgive us in the same manner and to the same degree that we forgive one another. That is really a very fearsome prayer, and it should drive us to our knees, crying out, "Father, help me to forgive others as you've already forgiven me."

God is dealing anew and afresh in the body of Christ with our relationships with one another. We're having to forgive people who seem quite unworthy of our forgiveness. Perhaps they have wronged us, and they have never said, "I'm sorry." They haven't repented because they haven't *been* sorry. They haven't cared if we never forgive them. But the Lord has been saying, "You forgive them anyway. I want your prayer channel to be a clear one so I can pour my blessing into you. That channel will be clogged as long as there's any unforgiveness in it."

Unforgiveness works like a cork in a tube. It's got to pop out before our channels of love and faith can be fully operable.

An unruly tongue. A tongue that is not under the Holy Spirit's control, a tongue that is used to express pride in one's own accomplishments and to gossip about other people, is not a tongue that can carry effective prayers to the Father. The one who can have meaningful fellowship with the Father in prayer is one who "backbiteth not with his tongue, nor doeth evil to his neighbour, nor taketh up a reproach against his neighbour" (Ps. 15:3).

The Christian who is always considering himself better than someone else, pointing the finger of shame, and keeping the pot stirred with "if you only knew what I know" innuendos shouldn't expect answers to his prayers. All that garbage completely clogs his channels of receptivity. It's as if God says to him (or her!), "Sorry you can't have what you've asked for in prayer. There's no opening through which I can grant the desire of your heart."

Another Scripture pointing to gossip as a hindrance to answered prayer is found in the book of Isaiah:

> Then, when you call, the Lord will answer. "Yes, I am here," he will quickly reply. All you need to do is to stop oppressing the weak, and to stop making false accusations and spreading vicious rumors! (Isa. 58:9, TLB)

Dishonesty. There is only one way to approach the Lord, and that is with complete honesty in everything.

God doesn't hold our past against us. He doesn't care what our past contains—unless we're lying about it. We can't come to the Lord saying, "Lord, you know I desire to do your will" if we don't desire His will at all. We can't fool God, because He's always looking on our hearts. He knows us far better than we know ourselves. But He doesn't mind our saying, "Lord, I confess I still want my own way in this. Please make me willing to want your way. Make me willing to be willing for you to change me."

God doesn't hold our present against us either, as long as

we're honest about it.

To all outward appearances, I was standing on the platform of a church one Sunday morning, praising the Lord in song: "Sweet Jesus, sweet Jesus." But inside, I was at home putting the roast on to cook.

"About 350 degrees, I think. And I'll bake some potatoes too. Wonder if they'll be done by 1:15—"

With my eyes closed, and my hands raised, my lips sang, "You're precious, more precious than gold." But my mind was still in the kitchen at home, thinking about what kind of salad to fix.

"Not only am I more precious than gold, I'm even more precious than dinner," the Holy Spirit reminded me.

Instant repentance hit me.

"I'm sorry, Lord. You are so right. I'll stop taking thought about what the day might bring. I'll worship you now." We sang the song again, "Sweet Jesus, sweet Jesus, what a wonder you are . . ." and this time my heart was agreeing with my mouth. As I stood in honesty and sincerity before God, I felt His blessing rain down upon me.

A *husband-wife relationship that is out of order* really disrupts our prayers:

> Likewise, ye wives, be in subjection to your own husbands; that, if any obey not the word, they also may without the word be won by the conversation of the wives. . . . Likewise, ye husbands dwell with them according to knowledge, giving honour unto the wife, as unto the weaker vessel, and as being heirs together of the grace of life; that your prayers be not hindered. (1 Pet. 3:1, 7)

If wives and husbands do not honor one another, their

prayers will encounter a bottleneck. And wives and husbands who pray with other people but not with each other give the enemy an opportunity to wreak havoc among those who are not aware of his devices.

When you begin to get serious about spending some time every day before the Lord in prayer, a softening process takes place within you. Your defenses come down as love flows through you in a way it never has before. And there is a tendency to pour out that love all over the person with whom you're praying. If that person is not your own husband or wife, watch out! You may feel such an affinity "in the Spirit" toward the one who has prayed with you, you'll disregard all the laws God has instituted for your protection.

Too many times I've had to pick up the pieces after two persons went overboard in an illicit relationship thinking it had the blessing of God just because they felt so religious and tender about it. All the tenderness in the world doesn't alter the fact that sin is sin. The Spirit of the Lord is telling us to watch out for such things, to keep our love for our brothers and sisters on a brotherly and sisterly level and not to fall into Satan's trap. Things can't get out of order when we won't let them get out of order.

Husbands and wives who succeed in praying together have a bond stronger than the most powerful glue. Together, they can put ten thousand foes to flight.

In many homes today, I see a spiritual teeter-totter. When the wife is up, the husband is down. When the husband is up, the wife is down. And instead of claiming the promise of Jesus, "If two of you shall agree on earth . . ." (Matt. 18:19), and appropriating the deliverance of the "down" one, they keep on tottering back and forth. This delights the enemy who knows that if he can keep them divided, he'll have broken the house asunder. Defeat or victory in the home is reflected in defeat or victory in the church and in the community.

God and I

Two working together *can* put ten thousand to flight. The devil knows that; that's why he tries so hard to keep husbands and wives from real unity in the Lord where they would know the strength of the power vested in them.

God is saying, "Don't cry to me unless you're going to meet the conditions I have laid down in my Word. But if you're going to meet the conditions, and get serious with me, I'll get serious with you." If we'll hear what He's saying and do it, we'll have power with God and power with men.

So much for the reasons our prayers are not answered. What are the positive conditions that insure answers?

1. We are assured of answers to our prayers when we confess His Word to Him.

> If ye abide in me, and my words abide in you, ye shall ask what ye will, and it shall be done unto you. (John 15:7)

The highest form of prayer is confession of God's Word.

"If my Word abides in you," God says, "you can bring it to me, and I'll honor it. You can ask what you will, and I'll do it for you."

"Thanks, Lord. Your Word says this—" Maybe we point out a specific promise having to do with healing or some other need in our lives.

"Is that what you want, Iverna?"

"Yes, Lord, I want it with all my heart."

"Then you shall have it," He will say. God works through the channel of His Word. He keeps His part when we keep ours.

2. Our prayers are answered when we ask for what we desire and believe that we receive it.

> Therefore I say unto you, What things soever ye

desire, when ye pray, believe that ye receive them,
and ye shall have them. (Mark 11:24)

This is such an incredible promise, that if we really believed
it, we'd be swinging from the chandeliers. We are to ask for
what we desire, and believe that we have it. We can trust the
Lord enough to ask Him for our heart's desire and know that if
the thing for which we are asking is wrong for us, He'll change
our desire. We are not the Lord of our prayer; He is.

At a conference one day, a woman came up to me and said,
"My husband and I need to know God's will about a certain
thing in our lives. We want His guidance in our decision."

Several people gathered round to help us praise the Lord
and to pray, "Lord, please let us know your direction for this
couple. We need an answer from you, and we believe you for
it."

As we waited before the Lord, a woman who had not heard
the specific prayer request came up to us with an open Bible
and got our attention.

"Do you have a word for us?" I asked her.

"I believe I do," she said, and she read aloud a passage that
was such a direct answer to the couple's need that day, it gave
us all goose bumps. The one who read the Scripture explained
to us afterward what had happened.

"Today I was just sitting with my Bible, having a 'listening to
the Lord' time," she said. "I had asked Him to show me His will
about some things in my own life and was just leafing through,
reading passages here and there as the Spirit led. When I
happened upon that particular Scripture, it didn't mean
anything to me, so I just read it and turned the pages and found
something that spoke to me. But the Lord seemed to say, 'Go
back and look that one up again and remember where you
found it.' I didn't know why He said that, but I was obedient,
and just now when I saw all of you praying about something, He

113

seemed to say, 'That Scripture I showed you? It's for them.' "

3. Our prayers will be answered when we seek wholeheartedly for what we need.

> And ye shall seek me, and find me, when ye shall search for me with all your heart. (Jer. 29:13)

When you know for sure what it is you want from God, you can begin to bombard the gates of heaven and know you will have what you ask for.

Some people today are teaching that once you ask God for a particular thing, you should never mention it to Him again, except to thank Him. They say you will know you have received it whether you can see it or not. I can't find any support for that teaching in the Word of God.

When Jesus advised people not to be like the heathen who made vain repetitions and piled up words by their much talking (Matt. 6:7), He was dealing with people who were praying with no understanding of what they were saying. He was not saying we couldn't ask God for something more than one time.

Some people can say the rosary, knowing why there are ten beads in each decade and what they're to focus their attention on while they're repeating each prayer. It can be very meaningful to them. But there are others who just breeze through, without even thinking about what the words mean. They seem to have little understanding of what they're doing. They're just doing their thing.

The Lord is saying, "They needn't think they're going to get anything for their vain repetition. I'm not impressed with it. If they're not listening, why should I?"

It was the Lord himself who told the story of the little woman who went before the unjust judge again and again and again. Finally, he got so disgusted with her, he gave up.

"Give her what she wants!" he ordered.

And the Lord tells us that if even an unjust judge will give in under repeated askings, what might we get from a just one (Luke 18:7)?

When we say with Jacob, "Lord, I want, I want, I want, and I will not let thee go, except thou bless me" (Gen. 32:26), God says, "I think she must mean what she's saying. That's about ninety-nine times in two days she's asked me. Gabriel, will you please send her one of those—the deluxe model."

4. Answers to prayer are forthcoming when we get someone to agree with us about what we're asking God for.

> . . . If two of you shall agree on earth as touching any
> thing that they shall ask, it shall be done for them of
> my Father which is in heaven. (Matt. 18:19)

Husbands and wives can pray together with power. Parents and children can agree together:

"Hey Deb, hey Dan, come here a minute. Agree with me, will you? I need to get ahold of God!"

I don't know why God set it up that way, but it works. In my own life, I'm alone a lot of the time—except for Jesus being with me. I've fought with the enemy for hours sometimes because it seemed like I was alone, but if I have someone with me who can join her faith to mine and believe God for victory over every power of darkness, there's always a difference.

There's still room for praying alone in a prayer closet, of course. Sometimes I need to be all by myself to pour it out to Him—and I might get loud—where it's nobody else's business and I don't want to be overheard. But you can pray "closet" prayers in a room with a thousand other people who are also offering up their petitions to God. I may hinder them a little, but they don't hinder me a bit. In the midst of them, I can close the closet of my mind—BAM!—and pray as if God and I are the only ones for miles around.

5. When a worshiper does the will of God, his prayers are heard.

> Now . . . if any man be a worshipper of God, and doeth his will, him he heareth. (John 9:31)

This promise carries a double blessing because the Scripture assures us in another place that any prayer according to God's will that's heard is answered:

> And this is the confidence that we have in him, that, if we ask any thing according to his will, he heareth us: And if we know that he hear us, whatsoever we ask, we know that we have the petitions that we desired of him. (1 John 5:14-15)

6. Our prayers are answered when we are walking in obedience.

> And whatsoever we ask, we receive of him, because we keep his commandments, and do those things that are pleasing in his sight. (1 John 3:22)

According to The Amplified Bible, the words here are speaking of our *habitual* practice of what is pleasing to Him. It is one thing to obey in a particular instance; it's quite another thing to walk in continual obedience. In a church service, I can sing, "Where He leads me, I will follow," and I will follow—until the service is finished.

Afterward, I may go outside and get in my car and head for home.

"I want you to turn left at this next corner, Iverna," He might say.

"But I always turn right, and I'm in a hurry to get where I'm going."

"I'm telling you to turn left. Remember the song you sang in church?"

"Of course, Lord. And I did follow you then. I really followed you. But right now, I want to take the direct route home."

He lets me have my way. I turn right. A few miles down the road, I come upon the biggest traffic snarl I've ever seen. While I wait and wait and wait for it to get untangled, I wish I had been obedient. If I had turned left, as He wanted me to do, I'd have been home five times sooner. Instant obedience, walking in conformity to His will for me, always has benefits.

I remember the first time God called on me to prophesy in the church. I was so scared.

"Lord, if this is really you prompting me to stand and speak forth your word, prove it to me by letting that little kid start crying."

"WAAAA! WAAA!"

The kid's mother took him out, and the Lord said, "All right. I honored your fleece. Now give the prophecy."

But my knees hadn't stopped shaking.

"Lord, if it's really you, let that kid come back in quietly now."

He glided down the aisle without making a sound.

"Now!"

But I had to prove Him some more, and finally, when I was afraid lightning would strike me if I delayed any longer, I got up and opened my mouth, saying, "Thus saith the Lord. . . ." The words just flowed. Oh, it was glorious!

At another service the Lord told me again to get up and speak forth the message He would give me. I started out the same way as before:

"Lord, if that's you—"

"Wait a minute!" He said. "Do you want me to use you or not?"

"Y-y-yes, Lord." I got up and gave the prophecy.

God is looking for each of us to come to the point of maturity where we can speak His Word to anybody at a moment's notice. He wants us to go about with a "Yes, Lord. Yes, Lord," attitude about everything, so that His will shall be done here on earth as it is in heaven.

I don't believe the angels argue over every little thing He asks them to do. They just do it. Can you imagine it being otherwise? Furthermore, He probably doesn't even have to tell them what He wants them to do. He just thinks it, and they do it. As we begin to have a "Yes, Lord. Thank you, Lord," attitude in our own lives, moving more and more into the perfect will of God, we'll know the heavenly benefits of walking in obedience right here on earth. When we meet the conditions, we can claim the blessings. The blessings are always there, but if we don't learn how to claim them, they don't do us much good.

7. Our prayers are answered when we ask in His name.

> And whatsoever ye shall ask in my name, that will I do, that the Father may be glorified in the Son. (John 14:13)

The righteousness of God demands that He be fair to every creature, even to Satan. I, who had been raised in righteousness, turned away from the Lord and did my own thing for two backslidden, wretched, rebellious years. When I tired of following my own way, which led me from one degree of misery to another, I turned back to the Lord, and He restored me to my original place in His family. I imagine that Satan went before the Lord and complained about it.

"It's not fair. Here you are, blessing the life of Iverna Tompkins again, anointing her, using her, being good to her, and it's not fair. She turned from you and chose to become one of mine. What right do you have to restore her to right standing with you?"

Jesus had an answer all ready. It was written in His Word.

"I had promised her," He said, "that if she would ask for anything in my name, she could have it. She asked."

9

Beware!

There are six general "bewares" of which Christians should be mindful when they pray for themselves as Jabez prayed.

1. *Beware of excessive enthusiasm.* Excessive enthusiasm can break you in pieces in spite of your prayer that it won't happen to you. I don't mean that you'll fall apart if you get too happy in His service; but some people, when they first become useful tools and vessels for the Lord, are so thrilled that He'll use them, they run night and day. After a few years, they break down and have to stay at home. It almost happened to me.

One day the Lord took me to task about it. "Iverna, you say I'm Lord of your life, but you haven't let me be Lord of your schedule."

My attitude had been, "If I book a meeting, I'll never cancel it." I hadn't realized that was unsurrendered pride until the Holy Spirit pointed it out to me. To me, it had sounded just, right, fair, and pure.

"Purer than any other minister, Iverna?"

"Well, yeah—" and then I saw what He was getting at.

"You don't give me a right to change your plans," He said.

I was so sick, I literally lay on the floor on my face before

God and I

God and said, "God, I don't know how to make you Lord of my schedule, but I hereby declare with my mouth that you are and shall be. Teach me how."

I haven't been totally popular with some people since then, but I'm a lot freer in Jesus. And how the Lord has managed! I've had to say no to this one, no to that one, and yes to a least likely one. But in it, He's saving me from the dangers of my own excessive enthusiasm.

2. *Beware of false burdens.* How do you know whether you're under a burden from the Lord or a false burden you've picked up for youself? *There is a way to know.* If your burden can be released in prayer—in an hour, a day, two or three days—it's probably from the Lord. "My burden is light" (Matt. 11:30), He said, and if a burden weighs you down, if you can't eat or sleep because of it, it's probably not one He recommends for you. What should you do in that case? Stop travailing for the burden and pray, "Lord, *your* burden is light, but this thing is very heavy. Release me in Jesus' name!" It will be done.

My mother has had quite a life of prayer. Several years ago, she was under a tremendous burden for one member of the family who was undergoing the dealings of God. How she travailed in prayer for him! I was a thousand miles away when the Lord spoke to me and said she was laboring under a false burden, one He hadn't given her.

"But God! That doesn't make sense. He's her son! Who's going to pray for him if she doesn't?" He reminded me that there *is* an Intercessor.

When I telephoned mom that night, I asked her how she was feeling.

"Not so good," she said. "I'm so concerned about one of the boys. My appetite is gone, I'm not sleeping well—things are bad."

"Mother, I'm going to believe God to release you from this burden. If it's a burden that someone here needs to carry, I'm willing to carry my part, and I'm going to pray that He'll put the rest of it on someone else. You need a vacation."

She agreed, we prayed together, and she was set free. It seemed that her burden hadn't come from the Lord after all—it just stemmed from the natural situation of a mother who had spent her life praying for her children. If they were in trouble she prayed them out of it. If they were out of trouble and growing too complacent, she prayed them into trouble. In this particular case, God was dealing with a young man who needed to be dealt with so that his mother's highest prayers for him could be answered, that he himself would grow into Christian maturity and act like it. Today, that man is being used of God, and his life is one with Christ.

Sometimes it seems that His easy burden is like birth pangs. I had a burden from the Lord for a certain man one day, and I literally groaned before the Lord for him for four hours. When I was finished, I knew I was finished. My stomach muscles ached for a week. But with that last pang, there was a birthing of something that released my inner spirit. Long before I ever found out what had happened, the Lord let me know the victory was *won*!

I believe in praying and groaning and sharing in the heart of God with our fervent concern. But it's not the will of God for the enemy to make us lose sleep, skip meals we need, or be so under a burden we can't function in our jobs. Such burdens are not from on high.

3. *Beware of becoming people-pleasers*. We dare not be ministers unto man, because if we are, we cannot be ministers unto the Lord. If I'm motivated by what people think instead of by the Spirit of the Lord, I'll get my orders from man, and nobody will be helped.

Some people today are in churches where the pastor has taken a hard-nosed stand against the moving of the Holy Spirit. Take a long look at why you're in such a church. If God set you there, when did He do it? Was it before you knew there was such a thing as the Baptism in the Holy Spirit and what it means to worship the Lord in spirit and in truth?

I don't believe in stagnating. Neither does God. I don't believe in going to a church that doesn't feed me with the Word of God.

"Well," people argue, "God put me here. What will people think if I leave?"

That's not the issue. Ask yourself, "Is my life making a difference in this place? Is God using me here to reveal to the church and its pastor that there is a flow of life in the Spirit of God? Or am I just drying up with the rest of the congregation?"

If your answer to that last question is yes, maybe you ought to do something to change it. Stop quenching the Holy Spirit in you.

Don't be afraid to pray for the sick just because your pastor doesn't do it. Don't be afraid to prophesy because your pastor doesn't encourage it. Be willing to do these things anyway, and let the results speak for themselves. I'm not suggesting that you interrupt a service or disobey leaders, but that you remain sensitive to the Lord, and as He gives opportunities, let His life flow through you to produce life in other members of the congregation. As that happens, people will be filled with the presence of Jesus, and they will be liberated from all that binds them.

When your pastor notices that your Sunday school class is the only one that's growing by leaps and bounds, and when he begins to glimpse that the anointing flowing through your life is greater than anything he can see in any other teacher, his eyes may be opened to the reality of what you're talking about. Why, he might ask to be filled with the same Holy Spirit himself!

Stay in a dead church only if God is using you there to impart life to His people. When the church you attend demands from

Beware!

you a denial of the Holy Spirit, be prepared to move rather than to quench the Spirit. God will release you and direct you to another segment of the body where you can be blessed and bless.

As a counselor and then a supervisor in probation work for five years, I got by with a lot of things. I violated more county rules than they had—almost. New staff members used to look on in awe and say, "How did you get by with *that*?"

"Because it works," I'd tell them. And I never got called on the carpet for my unorthodox methods. When nobody else could capture a runaway girl, they'd put me on the case. I'd get in my car and go out and check through the grapevine of all the Hell's Angels and everybody else. I'd find the kid and bring her back.

"Where was she?" the probation people would want to know.

"Can't tell you."

"But you can't keep a secret like that. You're a counselor—you represent the whole probation department."

"Next time you lose a girl, call me," I said, and they did. They might not like my methods, but they couldn't argue with the results. And results were what they were really after. God's after results when He puts His Holy Spirit in us too.

4. *Beware of legalism.* Whenever there is a move of God in the church, man comes along and tries to divert it, ignoring the Spirit and trying to bring it under his own control which always takes them back under the law.

Recently I received a letter of inquiry from a pastor who trusted my walk with the Lord.

"But," he went on to say, "I'm getting a lot of flak from people who think you're out of order when you're praising the Lord in tongues in a public service. They point out that the Scripture is very clear that any tongues in a public service must be interpreted."

I wrote him back saying, "Tell them when I'm praising in

tongues, I'm praising God, not talking to people. I don't care if they understand it or not. They shouldn't be listening."

People tend to get legalistic about prophecy too.

"Three prophecies and that's all," they insist. "That's what the Bible says."

I tell them what I have observed: it takes about twelve prophecies in some churches to equal one in another church.

In other cases, someone will find the Scripture that tells the women to have their heads covered when they prophesy (1 Cor. 11), and right away he'll require the women to wear little hankies on their heads, missing the whole meaning of what Paul was really saying, which was, "Let the women be under some kind of headship and supervision."

Legalism can make us shut out the presence of the Lord who set us free and can cut us off from fellowship with people who don't believe exactly like we do.

I know a pastor who drank wine with his dinner. Someone saw him, reported him to his denomination's headquarters, and the pastor was called on the carpet and warned, "If you drink wine again and we find out about it, you're through!" This happened in spite of the fact that the pastor had a flowing, growing congregation, and his use of wine with his dinner had never constituted a problem in his life.

We're to refuse the bondage of legalism. If you can't drink wine, don't try. But don't interfere with the man who can.

There is an inverse legalism, too, where one person attempts to do what God has forbidden for him, just because someone else gets by with it. If God has said that you should use grape juice for communion, you'd better stick with it. You'd choke on wine.

If God has told you to pray for an hour a day, do it. That someone else might pray only an hour a week with a greater anointing does not mean that his pattern is for you.

God doesn't give His people a long list of dos and don'ts which is the same for everybody. He writes His law on our hearts, and what He writes on mine for me is different from what He writes on yours for you.

Paul wrote, "I can eat anything, I can drink anything, I can do anything, I can go anywhere. I walk with God everywhere I go, and I thank Him for everything I take into my body. I do nothing in excess; I am temperate in all things. Therefore, I am free from the law. But I had rather not do any of the things permitted to me if they could hurt my brother and cause him to stumble" (see 1 Cor. 10:28).

We all need to find the proper balance between legalism and the freedom Christ gives us.

5. *Beware of criticism.* When we give voice to criticism, it is strewn to the four winds like feathers from a broken pillow. If we repent, God will forgive us, but we'll never be able to gather up all the flying feathers of rumor, innuendo, and speculation spread abroad by our criticism.

When I was in the business world, I often criticized my superiors. I saw ways they could do things better and make more money faster and easier. I thought I could make better displays of merchandise than they made, and I never approved of their plans or their rules.

One day the Lord said to me, "Iverna, do you know why you're working *under* them instead of being in charge *over* them?"

"Why, no, Lord. I don't know. But I blame it on the fact that the system is so lousy—"

"It's because you are still finding fault all the time," He said.

Until we're walking in the other person's moccasins, we don't have all the facts at our disposal.

I was sitting on a platform with a pastor one day, listening to some young people sing and play musical instruments. I thought some of them were talented; others should have stayed at home.

The pastor must have read the unspoken criticism I was projecting at one of the young men.

"See that young man over there playing the guitar?" he asked me.

"Yeah."

"Let me tell you about him." He explained how the boy had been a dope addict, at the very bottom of things, and how the Lord had saved him and was giving him a ministry of praising His name in music.

My opinion about the youth changed from black to white because I saw where he came from, and what he was in the midst of becoming by the grace of God.

"Why, he's beautiful in the Lord!" I heard myself saying, meaning every word of it. Two minutes earlier, I had been wondering why anyone had let him be on the program.

We can't afford to be critical. We don't know all the facts. And our criticism can do irreparable damage.

Criticism is not the same as exhortation. Criticism only points to the negative. It doesn't result in improvement. Exhortation, on the other hand, has as its purpose the edifying of another. When other people see a problem in my life, they can come to me and say, "Iverna, I believe it would be beneficial to your life if you would. . . ."

Then, they don't just leave me there. They promise to pray *with* me and *for* me, to hold my hands up as Moses' hands were held up (Exod. 17:12), and to believe God can bring the improvement to fruition in my life. That's *exhortation*. And that's what Christians are to do for one another.

Criticism delays maturity; exhortation speeds it up. A critical spirit can spoil us, rendering us useless.

6. *Beware of discouragement.* In conflict, we're dealing with God, man, Satan, and ourselves. Paul was writing about conflict when he said:

> We are troubled on every side, yet not distressed; we
> are perplexed, but not in despair; Persecuted, but
> not forsaken; cast down, but not destroyed; Always

bearing about in the body the dying of the Lord Jesus,
that the life also of Jesus might be made manifest in
our body. (2 Cor. 4:8-10)

The Greek word translated "troubled" means being pressed;
there is pressure upon us. That we are not distressed under
pressure means we are not put into a place from which we
cannot move. Paul is saying there is a way out.

If we're not able to see the way out, we should get our eyes
off the problem and pray, "Lord, which way is out?" He'll
always answer us, "I am the way out. Follow me."

When we are perplexed, we are like a ship that's come into a
harbor and found it all cluttered so there's not a free, clear
passage. The ship's captain would be discouraged and in
despair if there was nowhere for it to go, but it can always go
back the way it came in. So it is with the Christian. He might
find himself in a strait, but there's always a way out.

"Lord, I'm distressed and perplexed," we can tell Him, "but
I praise God I can still move. Help me not to go down another
blind alley next time."

We all make mistakes everybody can see—marital mistakes,
business mistakes, mistakes with our children. And we make
other mistakes that don't show at first—secret sins, immorality,
uncleanness. . . .

We might think we're at the end of our rope, but there is
always a way out through the One who is the door.

When we have deliberately walked into a situation that isn't
pleasing to Him, we have to turn around and walk out, just as
deliberately. Praying that He will deliver us out of the bad
situation avails nothing in such cases. We have to turn around
and remove ourselves from it. That might involve confessing
before men, "Look, I made an awful mistake. I'm sorry, God's
forgiven me, and I want your help to get back on the right track
again."

When we are persecuted, we are being pursued. God's

pursuing us, the devil's pursuing us, other people are pursuing us, and we're pursuing ourselves. But we are not forsaken; we are not just dropped down someplace and forgotten forever. God's keeping His promise never to leave us nor forsake us (Heb. 13:5).

Somebody who feels totally let down, totally without hope, hollers, "Well then, why don't I feel His presence?"

"Because you don't believe He's there."

"Will I find faith on the earth when I return?" Jesus asks us. "Will I find any faith at all in my Word? When I said I'd never leave you nor forsake you, I meant it. You may take some blind alleys, you may fall into some ditches, you may enter some harbors that are locked to forward motion, but I'm still with you. Back up your ship and turn again to me, and you'll know my presence once more."

About then, we're ready to fall into His arms, knowing they're there.

"We are cast down," Paul says in this Scripture (2 Cor. 4:9), "but we are not destroyed." We are cast down when everything we touch falls apart, when our prayers reach only about an inch above our heads, when our praise doesn't ascend to God but echoes in our ears as if God doesn't want to hear it. Being cast down can be a pretty desperate state, but Paul reminds us that even then we are not destroyed. Unlikely as it might seem at the time, we're *not* about to perish.

Instead, God is accomplishing His purpose in all He does to us. He's trying to make the trial of our faith precious to us.

One time-tested way for us to get out of the doldrums of discouragement ourselves is to minister to another. In doing that, we'll find ourselves declaring the Word of the Lord.

"I believe God for you. I know the Lord is in your life, and He's anointed you for His purpose. He'll work this for your good, believe me."

As we declare the word of faith to another, it reassures *us* too. We begin to believe there is hope for our lives as well.

10

Diversionary Tactics

The enemy of our souls knows when we intend to pray. And he knows how serious we are about this intention. Sometimes when we say we are going to pray, he doesn't bother to interfere because he knows we have no real intention of following through with our plans. But when he knows that we don't intend to let anything stop us, he goes to all kinds of trouble to frustrate us.

Many Christians have no idea how much power there is in prayer. They don't have any comprehension of their positional authority with God. If they understood who they really are, in terms of their relationship with the Head of the universe, they would begin to exercise the authority God has given them. Jesus told His followers, "All power has been given unto me (Matt. 28:18, paraphrased), and now I give it unto you. You'll be able to do the same things I am doing, and even greater things (John 14:12, paraphrased). The Father has given glory to me, and I give that glory to you (John 17, paraphrased). There isn't anything you can't do as believers—heal the sick, raise the dead . . . (Mark 16:17-18, paraphrased). You can be more than conquerors over everything" (Rom. 8:37, paraphrased).

God and I

When we read the passages of Scripture that proclaim these truths, we're likely to think Jesus was talking to Oral Roberts or Kathryn Kuhlman, or Billy Graham. But He was talking to "ordinary" believers. As long as we think Jesus was talking to the super-saints, the enemy can almost relax, but not quite. He knows there's always a chance we will wake up one day to who we really are in Jesus. And if we ever wake up to the potential He has placed in us, the enemy will be in real trouble.

The enemy has a number of tactics to divert us from God's full purpose for our lives. In speaking of these devices, Paul said, ". . . we are not ignorant of his devices" (2 Cor. 2:11). Modern Christians, unfortunately, are often appallingly ignorant of the tricks the devil plays to keep us from working the works of God. He uses the same tricks he used in the first century, because they still work so well.

In the Garden of Eden, the enemy said to Eve, "Has God said that? Are you sure it was God who said such a preposterous ridiculous thing as that?" (Gen. 3:1, paraphrased).

He can actually get us to question the voice of God: "Well, I *thought* it was God who said it."

"Oh, be reasonable now," he entreats us. "Surely God wouldn't have said such a thing!" After the enemy gets us to question the Word of God, it's an easy step from there for him to get us to do our own thing instead of to fit in with God's best purposes for us.

Next, Satan is likely to make us question our standing with God.

"You didn't really receive any gift from God," he'll jeer. "It's all your imagination. Why, you're probably not even really a Christian."

Satan will do all he can to make us doubt that we have a real relationship with God. We'll deny everything we've ever received from God and begin to worry about our own salvation instead of working it out as we are commanded (Phil. 2:12).

If these age-old approaches don't work with a particular Christian, Satan has still another tactic. He can get us to exaggerate our devotion so that it becomes a stumbling block to ourselves and to other people. If it's good for us to go to church and worship God, he gets us going twenty-four hours a day. If praising the Lord with a community of believers is good, he talks us into thinking it's all right for us not to clean house, not to go to work, not be part of the larger community. He gets us to separate ourselves into little "bless me" clubs and pull the walls of separation around us—just us and the Lord, a select group.

But Jesus said we were to be *in* the world, and not *of* it (John 17). And if we're called to be the light of the world and the salt of the earth, we'd better stay around where we can do a little salt shaking, and a little beaming forth of the light of the Lord where it's most needed.

With Paul and Silas, the adversary used another diversionary tactic to try to get them off the track when they were on their way to a place of prayer. Satan recognized that these two were on a rather mature level of functioning in the Christian life. They knew how to pray; they knew who they were in the Lord Jesus; their positional authority as sons of the most high God was known to them. And so Satan sent an interruption:

> And it came to pass, as we went to prayer, a certain damsel possessed with a spirit of divination met us, which brought her masters much gain by soothsaying: The same followed Paul and us, and cried, saying, These men are the servants of the most high God, which shew unto us the way of salvation. And this did she many days. But Paul, being grieved, turned and said to the spirit, I command thee in the name of Jesus Christ to come out of her. And he came

out the same hour. (Acts 16:16-18)

Here were two men who had every intention of praying. They had started out to go to a place of prayer.

It is easy for Christians to *intend* to pray. I can just see Paul and Silas having a late cup of coffee together the night before, and Paul saying, "Silas, in the morning, I want us to get together and go to a place of prayer and spend some time there."

Silas might have have answered, "That sounds like a good idea. We ought to do that kind of thing more often."

While they were on their way, a girl began to follow them, crying out, "These men are servants of the most high God, which shew unto us the way of salvation." She kept doing this for a period of several days, following them everywhere they went.

What she was saying *sounded* right, but that doesn't mean it *was* right.

Many of the interruptions in our spiritual lives sound right too, without being God's best will for us. We may be on our way to a place of prayer when the interruption comes. It may be an urgent telephone call, a demanding knock on the door, a cry for help, or an invitation you can't graciously refuse. Each of the interruptions might sound all right; they may represent valid needs, but they may not be right for you. And they have a common result—they keep you away from the place of prayer, diverting your attention from the things of God to the things of the world.

I've had many pastors tell me that just as sure as they turn aside to go to a place of prayer, their secretary will buzz them with a varied assortment of urgent requests from the congregation. If the pastors don't have any intention of praying, they can work for hours without interruption.

The girl following Paul and Silas had a need, but the interruption was not one the Lord had sent. Through the gift of discernment, Paul knew that the interruption had not been sent by God. The best judge of human nature can be fooled, but the Holy Spirit is never deceived. Paul ignored the damsel for some time, but finally, he had had enough. He certainly didn't need someone tagging along after him proclaiming that he was a servant of the most high God—she could have meant any god. And so at last Paul turned around and spoke to the spirit in the damsel, commanding it to come out in the name of the Lord. The spirit came out immediately.

There are still demons at large today, and they do oppress people, including Christian people who haven't availed themselves of protection from demons by continual submission to God. But I have some strong negative opinions abut the ministries of exorcism and deliverance that are getting so much attention these days. I hear about some ministers holding a person down and casting sixteen thousand devils out of him by name, and I can't find any scriptural basis for it. As I see it, that is a diversionary tactic of the enemy to draw attention away from Jesus and focus it on himself. Jesus said, "If I be lifted up, I'll draw all men unto me" (John 12:32, paraphrased). He'll do the work himself if we'll give Him half a chance instead of turning ourselves into professional devil chasers.

For a time, I was closely involved with a church where people were brought from miles around to have devils cast out of them. One day it dawned on me that the people who were delivered at our prayer meetings were not coming back in their delivered state to grow in Christian maturity.

About the time I realized all this, I heard the testimony of another minister who had come to the same conclusion.

"I fell on my bed one day," he said, "and I told the Lord, 'I've cast demons out of so many people, I'm exhausted with it. Lord, why do you keep on sending them to me?' "

"Oh, but I'm *not* sending them," was the Lord's reply.

"That's when I knew it was the enemy himself who was

sending them," the man told me. "He didn't mind that we were casting the devils out. He knew that he could reinhabit the same people again as soon as they stepped outside our door."

Having learned these things, some of us handle the enemy in a different way. Now, when he comes in to disturb a meeting, we don't focus on him, we focus on Jesus. Recently, when the enemy was trying to disturb a meeting, I had the congregation begin to sing, "Jesus, there's something about that name."

A woman came forward to say, "I'm full of devils."

"No, you're not," I told her. Then I spoke to the evil spirit in her and said, "You're a liar." Speaking to the woman again, I said, "Jesus loves you, lady." By then, the congregation was sounding forth, "His name is wonderful." Before long, the woman was rid of her unwelcome inhabitants and was entering into glorious victory.

Had we handled the problem by focusing our attention on the enemy, we could have gotten rid of him for a season, but we'd have been exhausted.

"Oh, boy, we really got those devils out," we might have boasted. And Satan might have been just as glad as we were, proclaiming, "I sure got my share of the attention at the service tonight."

The Lord said that we are to first submit ourselves to God and then resist the devil and he will flee (James 4:7) We are authorized to tell him that he has no part of us, no place in our home, no place in our life. We can claim the protection of the blood of Jesus.

In the case we are considering in the Book of Acts, Paul didn't make a big production of deliverance. He had only to say, "Be still. I won't have this disturbance any longer," and the woman had to be silent.

When the demons had been cast out of the young woman who was following Paul around, she became useless to her masters who had been making a lot of money from her ability to foretell the future. Naturally, they were furious, and they went to the magistrates and complained about what Paul and Silas had done. The magistrates promptly followed through, tearing the clothes off the visiting evangelists and commanding that they be beaten. When Paul and Silas had been beaten with many stripes, they were cast into prison, where the jailer was under orders to keep them safely.

Then the Scripture says that the jailer, ". . . having received such a charge, thrust them into the inner prison [the smaller cells], and made their feet fast in the stocks" (Acts 16:24).

Suddenly, the place of prayer was changed for Paul and Silas.

Some people in that position would have stopped praying and started griping and complaining.

"There I was, just moving along in the center of God's will, minding my own business, and all of a sudden, all these awful things started happening to me. My clothes were ripped off my back, I was beaten unmercifully, and thrown into this horrible dungeon. I can't understand why it happened. There was no sin in my life—"

Usually, there will be a symphathizer alongside somewhere.

"I know, honey. I went through the very same thing. In my case, the affliction lasted for eighteen years"

All the excess sympathizing and commiserating wouldn't have made the prisoners feel one bit better. As it happened, Paul and Silas handled their catastrophe in a different manner.

Around midnight, Paul spoke out loud: "Silas, are you awake?"

"You've got to be kidding! How could anyone sleep in this position? Yeah, I'm awake, all right. What's on your mind?"

"I was just thinking it would be a good idea for us to begin to pray and praise the Lord together."

Paul seemed to be aware that all that had happened was somehow for their good, that God was not putting them through an endurance contest and taking pleasure in looking down on the agonies that were being inflicted on them, saying, "Look at my kids, will you? I've put them through all this and they still take it without complaining."

That would have been a pretty warped picture of the fatherhood of God. We fall into it sometimes. Maybe we go to bed at night saying, "Father, thank you so much for enabling me to survive the rigors of this day."

Survival is not God's goal for our lives. He is producing something in us, and He is expecting us to show forth the fruit in our lives, just as a husbandman comes back to the vineyard, expecting to pick a bushel of grapes. He gives us the gifts in the beginning to enable us to plow the ground and plant the seed and water it and watch it grow. Then He extracts fruit from us when it is time. Often, the fruit shows up during periods of imprisonment, famine, and hard times, instead of when things are going well for us.

The Bible says that the triumph of our faith is precious. When I come victoriously through a trial, I'm likely to be ecstatic. "I made it! I made it! Did you see me?" And never again does the same situation plague me with fear that I won't make it. If I've been through it once, I can go through it again, confident of the outcome the next time.

When Paul and Silas began to pray there in the prison, I don't believe they were praying for their release from that place. I believe they were continuing to pray about whatever they had planned to pray about when their journey to the place of prayer was interrupted. They probably continued to pray for Philippi in Macedonia, interceding on behalf of the needs of those people. It was an indomitable prayer, one that couldn't be hindered by the lateness of the hour or the wretched physical circumstances in which they found themselves—bruised, in pain, humiliated, their goals thwarted. Everything was negative, except that they knew that God was greater than the circumstances.

When we have learned to be indomitable in our prayer life, when we refuse to be hindered or thwarted or diverted from our prayer, real victory is sure to follow.

As Paul and Silas prayed, an earthquake shook the foundations of the prison. The foundations of that which would have held them were collapsed around them, and the prison doors were opened. Everyone's bonds were loosed.

When the jailer became aware that everyone's bonds were loosed, he reached for his sword. In those days, a jailer who let his prisoners escape was subject to awful torture if he didn't do himself in before the authorities got to him. There was no such thing as a jailer being bribed to let a prisoner go free. Bribes aren't of much use to dead men.

But Paul stopped the jailer before he had a chance to kill himself.

"Don't hurt yourself!" he shouted. "No one has gone. We're all still here. Not a prisoner has escaped. You have nothing to fear."

There were some in the prison who might have made their escape if they had realized they were really set free. Paul and Silas knew their deliverance was real, but they were so unafraid, they were in no hurry to leave the place. The same God who had seen to their release could keep them from being locked up again.

The jailer had a hard time believing that the prisoners were still in the prison, so he called for a light. Sure enough, the head count tallied with the number of prisoners for which he was personally responsible.

When the jailer had seen Paul and Silas by the light of the lamp, Paul said to him, "Now let me tell you about the One who caused all these remarkable things to happen."

The jailer was ready to hear the explanation, and so he took Paul and Silas to his home. When he had heard the Good News he turned to his wife and said, "Honey, get the kids out of bed.

This is for all of us." She did, and the whole household was saved that night.

Paul and Silas knew whom they believed, and they were persuaded that He was able to keep all that they had committed to Him—and more besides. Their prayers were prayers of faith in a living God, giving Him the right to act in their cause. And when we give Him that right, He is able to act with power on our behalf and on behalf of those for whom we pray. All the diversionary tactics of the enemy will profit him nothing.

11

Faith and Intercession

Many books have been written about faith, many articles and pamphlets. Many sermons have been preached on the subject, and many tapes filled up with words about what faith is. But the more I've read, the more I've heard, the less I've really known about faith.

During an interview a few years ago, Kathryn Kuhlman was asked about her faith.

"I don't know very much about faith," she said.

Yet we thought of her as God's woman of faith.

I don't know much about faith either. Sometimes, I've thought I had a lot of faith, and I've been brought up short by what happened when I relied on my faith.

My home is in California, but I travel to other parts of the country in my ministry. For years, almost every time I went to the east coast, I'd get sick. I didn't know whether it was because of the change in climate, the different time zone, or what. It might have been attributable to a little bit of everything. Whatever the cause, I got tired of it.

Finally one day it dawned on me that I didn't have to put up with all that distress and discomfort. I could just take my stand on the promises of God that He had already borne all my afflictions, so I wouldn't have to bear them for myself. Since I was healed by His stripes, I wouldn't have to be sick.

"Lord," I prayed, "I'm going to go east tomorrow, and this time, instead of getting sick, I'm going to claim your Word for divine health in every cell of my body. I'm really going to believe you for wholeness in every inch of me."

When I hit the east coast, I stayed up late at night, got up early in the morning, was out in all kinds of weather, took on extra meetings that weren't part of my original schedule, and kept going like a house afire for days without a sign of sickness.

One afternoon the manager of my tape library out in California telephoned me. In the course of the conversation, he said, "You know, Iverna, it's a funny thing, but during this trip we haven't had the burden to pray for your health that we usually have when you're on the east coast."

"Praise the Lord!" I shouted. "God has taken care of it. I believe I have finally obtained a measure of faith." He rejoiced along with me at my growth in the Lord, my ability to claim the promises of God.

The next morning, I woke up sneezing, my head stopped with a cold, a feeling of misery permeating my whole frame.

"What's happened, Lord?" I wailed to Him. "What went wrong? I thought I had faith this time for divine health, and just look at me! This is the sickest I've been for a long time."

As the week went on, I came to understand that what I had mistaken for a high level of faith was simply excitement over the fact that I wasn't ill.

I still believe in divine health for God's children, but apparently I have something more to learn before I can appropriate it fully for myself.

Faith is not simply a feeling that a thing is so. Sometimes I've prayed for ten people with varying needs at the close of a meeting. I might feel faith for seven of them and tell them they were healed. I'd pray for the others just as fervently, but not have any assurance they were going to get well. Later I might learn that the seven stayed sick, and the three were healed overnight.

I might pray a very fancy prayer, and nothing would happen as far as anyone could tell. I might pray the simplest of prayers, crying out, "Oh, my God!" and He'd take perfect charge of the situation and work everything out.

Prayer is based on who He is and what He has promised to do under certain circumstances, not on our faith or lack of it. And answers to prayer are also based on His Word and not on how we feel about it. And yet, when we see an unseen thing as reality, we can make it ours by faith. But if we don't see it, no amount of lip affirmation can make it come to pass.

I've learned that faith is not our ability to order God around, in Jesus' name, but His ability to order us around because we believe in what He says.

Faith is not presumption, although some people have been teaching just that. They teach us to say, "I don't have a headache. I don't have a headache. I don't have a headache." Then, in the agony of our pain, we've screamed out, "Doesn't *anyone* have an aspirin?"

Faith and presumption are two different things. Faith does not come by will power; faith comes by hearing the Word that our ears have been opened to receive. Faith is looking into the Word of God and having that Word quickened to us by the Holy Spirit, not by our grim determination. When we come to the point where we believe in our hearts, then we can truly say, "God, I believe that for me." At that point, the gift of faith has come to us, and the thing that isn't seen can be made visible in our lives.

Faith is not standing around talking about what God can do. Faith is appropriating His promises for our lives today.

All of us need to have our faith enlarged. When the disciples came to Jesus and said, "Lord, increase our faith," He told them how to do it themselves.

"You want faith?" He asked them. "Look at a grain of mustard seed. If you plant it and water it with the water of the Word, it will grow. You'll see it produce fruit in abundance."

Hearing the Word of God will increase our faith, and watching the Word produce fruit will increase faith too. The Lord is endeavoring to increase our faith when He leads us to ask for larger and greater things. He is making our steps of faith bigger.

I like to think of faith in its relation to our senses—hearing, tasting, seeing, touching, smelling. Faith comes by the ear that hears the promise; faith comes by the eye that sees fulfillment; faith comes by the hand that lays hold of us; faith comes by the mouth that declares the promises of God and tastes their sweetness. Faith comes by the nose that smells the fragrance of all that God has promised to His church.

That faith in God is absolutely vital to our life and well-being.

As the Greek word for faith (*pistis*) declares, faith is total reliance on the word of another.

"Lord, I believe; help thou mine unbelief" (Mark 9:24).

A woman came into my office one day just as the choir was gathering for rehearsal. She looked like death warmed over—simply awful. Her eyes were dark and saggy, her skin looked more dead than alive, her expression was full of emptiness. She sat down in the chair I offered her and poured out a tragic story.

While she was speaking to me, I was seeking the Lord for wisdom to know how to deal with her. He let me know, "This woman is without faith or hope."

She had told me that she had tried to commit suicide.

"I can't even be a success in getting rid of myself," she whimpered.

When she had finished her outpouring, I began to share my

faith with her, my hope in the Lord Jesus Christ, and somehow she was ready to take hold of that hope for herself.

"I'm going to believe God with you," she said. It was as if she was planting her hope on the Lord's steadfastness as He had revealed it to me, and by the time she walked out of my office, the change in her was so remarkable, the choir members who had seen her walk in could hardly believe their eyes.

"Was that really the same person?" a soprano asked me. I nodded.

"What happened in that office?" an alto said, but I didn't have to answer because she knew what a difference faith in a living God can make. It is the difference between life and death. It is the difference between having no hope and having abundant reason to be alive.

After Pentecost, Peter was a man of tremendous faith. Look at the account of his steadfastness:

> Now about that time Herod the king stretched forth his hands to vex certain of the church. And he killed James the brother of John with the sword. And because he saw it pleased the Jews, he proceeded further to take Peter also. (Then were the days of unleavened bread.) And when he had apprehended him, he put him in prison, and delivered him to four quaternions of soldiers to keep him; intending after Easter to bring him forth to the people. (Acts 12:1-4)

It looked as if Peter's life was coming to an end. But Herod was going to wait till Easter time to finish him off, having a trial and making a big scene of it because the people would be so thrilled to be rid of him.

> Peter therefore was kept in prison: but prayer was made without ceasing of the church unto God for

him. And when Herod would have brought him
forth, the same night Peter was sleeping between two
soldiers, bound with two chains: and the keepers
before the door kept the prison. (Acts 12:5-6)

I marvel at Peter, that on what was supposed to have been
his last night on earth, he just lay there in his cell, sleeping
peacefully. Most of us would have been pacing the floor, at
least, crying out to God for deliverance, but Peter had faith that
God had the victory already sewed up for him, and he didn't
need to lose any sleep over it.

In this Scripture, we find an answer for people who wonder if
they should keep on praying about a thing once they have
mentioned it to the Father. The church was interceding
"without ceasing" for Peter while he was in prison. In such
cases, continual intercession is clearly called for.

Night and day, the people of the church in Mary's house, the
home of the mother of John and Mark, remained in a prayer
meeting, interceding on behalf of the imprisoned, endangered
Peter. "Lord God, our beloved Peter is in prison. The
authorities are planning to kill him, Lord."

I don't suppose any of them told the Lord *how* to bring about
Peter's rescue. They just asked God to have mercy on His
servant Peter, knowing that He could figure out a better way to
do it than anything they might propose.

We make a grave mistake when we try to tell God how to
answer our prayers. He has already told us:

For my thoughts are not your thoughts, neither are
your ways my ways, saith the Lord. For as the
heavens are higher than the earth, so are my ways
higher than your ways, and my thoughts than your
thoughts. (Isa. 55:8-9)

All pray-ers need to let this Scripture sink into their consciousness because most of us have a tendency to put off praying for some things until we have figured out how we want Him to act in the matter. We have a problem; we look at the problem and figure out how He can resolve it; and only then do we pray about it.

"Lord, I've considered this from every angle. If you go this route, that will hurt so-and-so. As I see it, these are your options, and I recommend this way because—"

"Iverna, do you really want me to handle this?"

"Of course, Lord. I know you have the power to do it, and I know that with your omniscience, you could figure out how to do it exactly right, but I've already checked the map, and—"

When I see He isn't buying my system, I finally get the point.

"All right, Lord. I give you the moral right to do it your way." He does it in some way that had never entered my head, always a better way than anything I had dreamed up. His ways are *not* our ways; they're always better.

Sometimes we've had something against another person and wanted the Lord to take vengeance on him.

"You get even, Lord," we tell Him. Maybe we even show Him the Scripture that says, "Vengeance is mine; I will repay, saith the Lord" (Rom. 12:19) just to prove that He's the one who's supposed to take action against our enemy.

One time I tried that, and I could hardly wait to see how the Lord would treat the fellow who had done me wrong. I was hoping He'd really zap him. I even watched the newspaper headlines for the report on it, almost holding my breath with the waiting. I felt extremely righteous in the whole thing, praying fervently, "Vengeance is yours, O Lord. I'm not going to do anything against this person. You go get him, Lord."

As I continued to pray, I found something happening to me. I'd hear myself saying, "Lord, I don't care what you do to him—but whatever it is, make sure it will correct his way and set him on a right path in your sight."

The Lord seemed to receive that prayer with an attitude that said, "We'll wait a little while longer. Iverna's making progress in the right direction. She's getting there."

Eventually the day came when my heart was so filled with the love of God for the man that I prayed, "O Lord, I hope you'll really get ahold of him and help him to know your love. Don't pour out your judgment on him, O Lord, but show him your mercy."

When I had reached that point, the Lord acted. He poured out His mercy on the man in such an overwhelming way that his life was transformed.

I had learned something more about the ways of God. He had taken vengeance out of my heart and fulfilled the perfect balance of righteousness in His judgment and mercy in the life of that man. That perfect balance is found only in the action of God. When we Christians try to get into the act, we go overboard one way or another. We do our righteous judgments without mercy. We do our mercy without righteous judgment. But God strikes the perfect balance and does everything just right.

His ways are *so* much higher than our ways, but we are learning to commit our ways unto the Lord.

If the Lord would choose to go along with my ways, I'd let Him. I wouldn't mind at all. But that's not how He chooses to work in my life. I have to say, "Lord, I'm yours. You bought me with a price, the blood of Jesus. Have your way in me."

By their repeated prayers, the people of the church were showing that they had real compassion on Peter in his plight. Compassion might be described as co-passion, a fervent caring for someone, caring such as Jesus felt when He had compassion.

Christians are commanded to "put on bowels of mercies"

toward one another (Col. 3:12). The phrase refers to the womb of our being, the portion of us which can literally travail and bring forth something.

Today we seem to have lost such depth of caring, such passionate yearning concern for one another. We have become careless, even almost flippant in our attitudes about many things.

Someone will come to us, broken with grief, because a loved one's illness has just been diagnosed as terminal cancer. Then they'll ask us to pray for the sick person.

"Sure," we'll say, our minds being a million miles away from any real concern for the sick person. Then, without even bothering to come into the presence of the Lord in the way prescribed in the Scriptures, we might say, "Lord God, our Father, we lift to you for healing this person—"

Turning to our informant, we ask, "What did you say his name was? And what did the doctors say was wrong with him?" proving that we weren't really concerned about the person or his ailment. There's no way we will persevere in prayer, or pray fervently or effectually with that kind of a beginning, with that lack of concern.

But we cannot muster up concern if it isn't there. We have to pray, "Lord, help me bear this burden with your compassion. Let me feel what you feel for this person." Such a prayer is liberating in its effect. It spares us from the guilt that follows unconcern.

Perhaps someone comes with a terrible need you know the Lord Jesus can meet, but when you pray, your prayer doesn't get beyond the ceiling. All day you berate yourself for your lack of compassion, your utter lack of involvement and concern.

You can avoid all that agony by making Jesus the Lord of your prayer life.

"Lord, are you concerned for this home? Is this your hour, is this your time to do something about it? Is this a burden you want to be part of my life just now?"

As you ask, He will give you what He wants you to have—a real concern in your spirit, a divine flooding of the energy of faith, an energizing that will enable you to pray in victory.

I've had this work in me to such an extent that I've been able to look right into the face of the foe and laugh because I could see God had already done the work. I just knew the thing was accomplished even though it was too soon for the results to be manifested in a way the natural eye could see.

I've seen people come forward in a prayer line, deep needs etched in the lines of their faces, and I've had to stifle joyful laughter because the Lord was saying to me, "See that brother? See that sister? I care about them, and I'm going to undertake to do mighty things in their lives. The enemy of their souls is on his way out already."

Today, we're more aware than ever before that we are wrestling not against flesh and blood but against principalities and powers and rulers in high places of darkness. We're aware of strongholds over lives, families, homes, and communities. These strongholds of the "strong man" can be broken by intercessory prayer. When we have done and said all of the things we know to say and do and the situation remains unchanged, it pays us to take a second look and see if the Lord isn't demanding a higher expression of faith from us. I have heard myself rise to that level of faith and pray, "Lord, there is a bad situation in this home. I bind the strong man in the name of Jesus, and I take authority over him and claim the victory in the name of Jesus."

After I've heard myself pray that prayer, I've seen miracles happen, situations change, persons be set free by the power of God.

Faithful intercession, in the fullest sense of the word, is on its way back to the church of the Lord Jesus Christ, but it will never come as long as we're content to remain in a judging attitude and find fault with everything that goes on in the life of the church. How much time we have wasted in criticism and condemnation.

"Oh, I wish the Lord would show her this"; "I wish the Lord would show him that"; "I wish the Lord would shut this one up"; "I wish the Lord would turn that one on."

When we see that things are out of order, our proper role is not to spread tales about imperfections but to keep our mouths shut except when we're in our prayer closet. There we can say, "Lord, I know you're concerned about this one, that one, and the other one. I'm opening myself to you as a channel of intercession for them. I'm giving you the legal right to act in their lives by bringing them to you in prayer."

Often we will find ourselves interceding when the person for whom we're doing so much praying doesn't seem the least bit concerned about his plight. The natural tendency in such a case is to exert our selfishness, sputtering an exasperated, "Well, if he's as unconcerned as all that, I'm sure not going to waste *my* time worrying about him." Or maybe, "I thought she had such an awful problem, but she's not down here praying it through, so why should I bother?"

But look at Peter. He couldn't be really comfortable, chained between two soldiers, but he was making the best of it, snoring away, while the church was praying without ceasing for him. It often happens like that—the person in the visible ministry is undergirded by the prayers of those who labor behind the scenes. Don't set your limits: "I'll pray for them only if they'll pray for themselves." Pray when the Lord of pray-ers and of prayers gives you a burden for someone. Different parts of the body have different functions at different times, and the Lord will show you which part He has appointed for you today.

Just as no good marriage is a balanced fifty-fifty proposition at all times, there are changing relationships in the body of Christ. In a marriage, maybe for a while the husband seems to be doing all the giving in, letting her have her way about things. And then, all of a sudden, things are the other way around. She's catering to him about everything. The ratio may look like ninety-ten for a while, then it might veer to the opposite ninety-ten. It's only on an average—if then—that fifty-fifty seems to apply. In the church, you may spend all your time interceding for others for a certain period; then you may be in the front line with the whole church interceding for you. He has chosen to make us mutually interdependent in a lot of things. "Bear ye one another's burdens," He tells us, "and so fulfil the law of Christ" (Gal. 6:2).

The burden for real intercession is a terribly gripping one. One time I chanced to learn about something offbeat in the life of one of God's highly exalted servants. If the thing became openly known, it would destroy his ministry. I knew I couldn't go to the man and confront him with it, and I certainly had no right to go to anyone else. I went to the only place open to me; I went to the Lord about it.

"Lord, I don't know why you've let me know this thing, but you must have had a good reason. You must want me to intercede for him."

I began to pray a prayer of intercession, daily calling that man's name in prayer, bringing him before the Lord. As I did that, it seemed that that man's life was my total responsibility, that what happened to him was in my hands, just as if he had been a tiny baby placed in my care. I prayed all I knew to pray in English; then I let the Holy Spirit pray through me because I knew I didn't know what to pray for as I ought. After I had travailed for him for a few days, I heard myself praying an unbelievable prayer from the depths of my heart:

"Almighty God, if there has to be a penalty, even the penalty of a life for the wrong that has been done, please take my life for his. I gladly lay myself down, Lord. My life is far less influential than his. Punish me and not him, Lord."

In the natural, I didn't care that much about what happened to the man. But Jesus cared that much, and that was the whole point of the burden of intercession that had been placed on me. The compassion of Christ was coming through a human vessel. It continued to come through me for that man for four whole months. Every day when I went to prayer, I would find myself groaning for that man. After the four months were up, the burden was lifted. Later I learned God had wrought a victory in that man's life, and I have felt ever since that I have been a part of his ministry.

He has no idea I had any part in God's mercy to him, but the Lord and I know. Every once in a while, when someone mentions his name, I have to say, "Glory to God! We did it!"

That kind of faithful intercession is something we'd never enter into without a specific calling of the Holy Spirit. There's no way a person could muster up that kind of devoted concern and stay with it for that length of time unless God was in it.

I've had people tell me, "The need is the call," saying that every need of all mankind is our personal call to pray for the persons involved. I have to argue with them about that. If I took every need of which I am aware to be God's call on my life for continual intercession until that need was met, I'd never have time to breathe. If every need was God's call to me, I'd drop dead tomorrow. I don't dare open the appeals that come in the mail with the pictures of starving orphans, because I want to adopt every one of the kids. My heart goes out to them.

"I'll take that one and that one and that one." I just don't have any sense about such things.

I'm called to every mission field I see pictured in magazines. There's a natural drawing there, without discrimination. I'd have to be split up into a thousand pieces to go to all of them. That's how I know the need isn't the call—at least not for me.

How can we handle these things? I compensate by praying for every need that's brought to me personally with a request for prayer. But I don't promise to keep on praying about that need forever; I promise to pray only when the Holy Spirit brings it to my remembrance. Some needs He brings back often to my mind, and I intercede again and again. For others, after the first prayer is finished, I never think of the particular need again. And I don't bother to ask the Holy Spirit why He hasn't reminded me to pray for this one or that one every day. I assume He's a better bookkeeper than I could ever be.

There have been times in my own life when I was quite aware that someone was interceding for me. Once when I was attempting to walk away from the "women in the ministry" syndrome, I resigned from a church position and went into business for myself. I won't go into the awful details, but during the next eight months, I went through literal hell. I lost everything—my home, my health, my job, my security, and almost my sanity. At the end of that time, when I was struggling to find myself again, I attended a joint World Map–Elim Bible Institute camp meeting. Standing in the registration area, I spotted a man I knew by sight, though he did not know me. He tipped his head in my direction and asked someone (I lip-read his question from across the room), "Who is she?"

"Judson Cornwall's sister," the person replied. (I was able to lip-read that too.)

The little man with the big moustache and the tambourine was Costa Deir. He walked over to me immediately and introduced himself. Then he said, "I don't know you, but I know you're Judson Cornwall's sister, and I could tell you what you've been through during this last year. God brought your face to me while I was in Africa and again in Jerusalem. I literally experienced physical pain that you endured, sister. I went through the mental agony you suffered this past year, and it was my privilege to bear you up before the throne. I'm so grateful to God that He let me be a part of it."

That was another example of intercessory prayer inspired by the Holy Spirit. When our prayers are inspired by the Holy Spirit, they're heard by God the Father, and they are answered.

Still another example of intercession inspired by the Holy Spirit came to me one night when the Lord brought a strange word to my mind, a word I'd never heard—"Tanganyika." The word was so forcibly in my mind, I had to take it before the Lord. It sounded like a disease to me, so I prayed, "Lord, whatever this thing is, I ask you to deliver it, in Jesus' name." After I had prayed in the Spirit for a while, the name faded from my consciousness, and I went to sleep.

A few days later, I attended a meeting in which representatives from a place named Tanganyika were called on for a report. Their report had to do with a political uprising that had threatened the lives of some of their people a few days earlier. The uprising happened at the same time the Lord stirred me up to pray for the strange-sounding name.

When we are living as children of the King, full of the faith that comes from knowing who we are in the Lord, God is able to trust us so much that He can actually share His own heart with us. It's as if He is asking us to open a legal pathway, by prayer, which He can use to intervene in the lives and affairs of His people.

As the saints prayed for Peter, God moved in a mighty way:

> And behold, the angel of the Lord came upon him, and a light shined in the prison: and he smote Peter on the side, and raised him up, saying, Arise up quickly. And his chains fell off from his hands. And the angel said unto him, Gird thyself, and bind on thy sandals. And so he did. And he saith unto him, Cast thy garment about thee, and follow me. And he went out, and followed him; and wist not that it was true

which was done by the angel; but thought he saw a
vision. (Acts 12:7-9)

Peter, the great man of faith, thought his eyes were
deceiving him. "Man, this can't be true!" he might have said if
he had lived in the twentieth century. "I'm not really seeing an
angel—an angel didn't really come in and wake me up. It's all
my imagination. I've been working a little too hard lately."

Almost every Christian has had the experience of praying
and praying for a thing, seeing it come to pass, and being
unable to believe that God really heard, and God really
answered. "This can't really be the Lord," we tell ourselves.
"There just has to be a natural explanation for it."

In verse ten, we read that Peter and the angel went past the
first ward, or guard post, and then the second one.

When we get through the first imprisonment of our lives, we
are likely to say, "Yeah, but that was just coincidental—really
no sovereign intervention of God there at all." As we approach
the second iron gate, representing access to freedom from
another thing that has bound us, we may look at the bars and
despair, complaining, "This is it. I know I got through that
other trial, *maybe* with a *little* bit of help from the Lord, but it
was mostly my own efforts, after all. So I'm not looking for God
to get me though this one either. It looks like the end of the line
for me. That iron gate is so tall and formidable. There's no way
I'll ever make it over. It will just keep on sealing up the rest of
my life."

Then suddenly, we hear a loud squeak and we watch the gate
swinging open with no effort on our part at all. This time, we
know it just *has* to be God!

But you say you wouldn't know where to go if God opened
the final door of your imprisonment? Neither did Peter, but he
didn't have to know anything. God had an angel there to get
him started on the next stage of his journey.

After the angel had left him, Peter said, "Now I know of a surety that the Lord sent His angel to deliver me out of the hand of Herod" (Acts 12:11, paraphrased). And Peter was so excited with that knowledge, he didn't go anywhere for a while. He just stood there in the street, praising God. "God, I really believe that was you. Thanks for coming into my life in such a miraculous way. It's marvelous, Lord, simply marvelous, and I really appreciate all you're doing for me."

I've known people who were set free by the Lord who have kept on standing in the middle of the street for over twenty years. When they have an opportunity to testify, they say, "I thanked the Lord twenty years ago for delivering me. He loosed the chains that bound me, opened wide the iron gate, and I stepped out into the path of God."

Everybody groans, "Oh, no, not again. We've heard that testimony a million times at least. Won't she ever have anything new to say?"

I always want to interrupt the testifier and say, "So you stepped out into the path of God twenty years ago? Wonderful! What has happened since then?"

I always imagine they'll have to admit, "Well, nothing, exactly. I'm still standing there on the path."

When Peter finally came to himself, he went to the house of Mary, the mother of John. Many people were still there praying, and when Peter knocked on the door, Rhoda answered it.

"Yes, who's there please?"

"It's I, Peter."

"Glory to God!" Rhoda shouted. "God's answered our prayer, everybody!"

She was so excited, she forgot to unlock the door. Sometimes we do the same thing. We get so excited that God is answering our prayers that we forget to open the door and let the answers come inside.

God and I

When Rhoda tried to tell the rest of the pray-ers that their prayers had been answered, that Peter was standing outside, they couldn't take time to listen.

"Oh, people!" she said. "I have the best news for you—"

"Sh-h-h, Rhoda. Can't you see we're praying?"

"But you don't understand. Peter is—"

"Rhoda, honestly. We need quiet to concentrate—"

"But Peter's *here!*"

"What do you mean, 'Peter's here'? Now, honey, faith is one thing, but you mustn't pretend that a prayer is answered just because—"

"But I *saw* him! Peter *is* here! He's standing outside the gate!"

"Rhoda, examine your heart. Are you sure you're telling the truth?"

"Cross my heart."

"Folks, Rhoda has just seen a ghost."

Well, she continued to carry on, so just to humor her, someone finally listened, and sure enough, there *was* a knocking at the door.

Peter was still at it because he had no place else to go. He wanted to get in so badly that he kept on knocking. Some people think the whole point is the knocking, and they are cheated out of a lot of blessings.

"Well," they'll say, "I did my knocking today. Really spent some time seeking the Lord."

"Good! Did He open any doors for you?"

"Oh, I couldn't say about that. I did my knocking and then got back to work. I didn't have time to hang around to see if my knocking did any good or not."

The people praying for Peter's release went to the door and were astonished to see that Peter *was* there, really Peter, and not his ghost. They let him in, he told them all that had happened, gave them instructions about what they were to do next, and then took off for his next assignment.

In the church, the accomplishment of one thing often spells defeat for the people because they are not quick to move on to the next assignment God has for them. I have seen churches come together in a beautiful way for a building program. Everything goes along so wonderfully—people give their money, their time; the flow of love is almost tangible; the women pray for strength for the men. It's a beautiful body ministry, and at last it's time for the dedication. All arrangements are made, the day dawns bright and beautiful, everything is glorious. But when that service of dedication is over, the Spirit is gone, and everyone gets the blahs.

What's the problem? It wasn't that the people got proud of their building, but that they didn't know how to receive an answer to prayer and then go on to a new opportunity. They had been geared to their goal instead of to the One who set the goal for them and enabled them to meet it.

We're not to consider ourselves specialists, building-builders whose whole life's work is done when the first building is completed. We're to know Christ has given us faith for a whole variety of things in line with His will. When the building is finished, we should praise the Lord and wonder what He's going to do next. We're not to take a sabbatical or limit ourselves to one phase of operations. If we want to function in real kingdom living, we have to keep on knocking at every door He wants to open for us.

In God's church today, there seem to be a lot of specialists. I hear ministers telling other ministers, "My ministry is healing, what's yours?" Or, "My ministry is teaching about the gifts, what's yours?"

I don't belittle any specialized ministries, but I don't have one. My calling is to the Lord Jesus Christ. I believe that the Holy Spirit within me is *the* gift, and every operation of the Spirit through me is the best gift for the particular situation with which I am confronted. He is faithful to give me faith for everything in which He wants me to trust Him.

12

Supplication for Successful Saints

For years we've been told to pray for sinners. That's unscriptural. The Bible tells us to ask God for the heathen, and He will give them to us for our inheritance. He doesn't ask us to pray that He will bless them. Instead of praying for souls, we are instructed to pray the Lord of the harvest that He will send forth laborers into His harvest (Matt. 9:38), that He may reap His reward. Since I don't know who is going to come to know the Lord, I am to show love and kindness toward everyone, to walk before all persons in such a way as to demonstrate Jesus Christ to them. It is not my responsibility to win all men, but it is my responsibility to be Christ-filled before all men.

The Bible has very few references where anyone is told to pray for unbelievers. It is true that Abraham spoke to God on behalf of Sodom, but he was pleading that God would spare the city for the sake of the righteous men in it, not the unbelievers of the city. And it is true that Paul travailed in behalf of the whole Jewish race and nation, praying that they might all be saved. But that was a rather unique instance in Scripture.

Jesus said, "Father, I pray not for the world. I pray for mine and yours" (John 17:9, paraphrased). All through the Word, we are encouraged to follow His example, to pray for one another, to pray for believers, to lift up the hands of holy men everywhere, to get ahold of God for one another.

When I began to think about these things as the Lord brought them to my attention, I didn't understand at first.

"God, do you mean that we are not to be concerned about souls?"

"No, Iverna, I don't mean that. You *are* to be concerned about souls. But you are to express your concern in a different manner. When the church of the Lord Jesus Christ is rightly related to Christ, when He is Lord of every area of your life, you won't have to worry about the lost being saved, because they will be won through your chaste conversation (1 Pet. 3:1-2), and your divinely inspired, love-filled life among them."

Generally, we feel that it would be easier to pray for the lost than to win them by our example. But that's not how it's done, God says. The enemy has tried to divert our prayers to purposes for which they were never intended instead of letting us pray for fellow believers. But the church is beginning to respond to God's plan, and is recognizing that we have to pray for one another because He is calling us to a degree of maturity we can never attain on our own. He himself is continually making intercession for us (Heb. 7:25).

We are a crisis-oriented people, and God wants to deliver us from that. We pray for people who have cancer, heart attacks, broken marriages, unemployment. If somebody wants us to pray for them, they must have a problem in order to be qualified. Sometimes we have been so diligent in praying for the heathen and in praying for persons in crisis situations that we haven't had any time left over to pray for believers. And yet there has never been a time when there was more need for the saints to pray for one another than there is today. The men and women of God need our prayers when they're successful, when they're prospering, when the Holy Spirit is moving through their lives, when their families are all together, when they're in perfect health, when they're walking in the Spirit.

Paul recognized these things when he wrote to the Colossians. He had spotted a group of successful Christians, and he prayed for them night and day:

Paul, an apostle of Jesus Christ by the will of God, and Timotheus our brother, To the saints and faithful brethren in Christ which are at Colosse: Grace be unto you, and peace, from God our Father and the Lord Jesus Christ. We give thanks to God and the Father of our Lord Jesus Christ, praying always for you, Since we heard of your faith in Christ Jesus, and of the love which ye have to all the saints, For the hope which is laid up for you in heaven, whereof ye heard before in the word of the truth of the gospel; Which is come unto you, as it is in all the world; and bringeth forth fruit, as it doth also in you, since the day ye heard of it, and knew the grace of God in truth: As ye also learned of Epaphras our dear fellowservant, who is for you a faithful minister of Christ; Who also declared unto us your love in the Spirit. For this cause we also, since the day we heard it, do not cease to pray for you, and to desire that ye might be filled with the knowledge of his will in all wisdom and spiritual understanding; That ye might walk worthy of the Lord unto all pleasing, being fruitful in every good work, and increasing in the knowledge of God; Strengthened with all might, according to his glorious power, unto all patience and longsuffering with joyfulness; Giving thanks unto the Father, which hath made us meet to be partakers of the inheritance of the saints in light: Who hath delivered us from the power of darkness, and hath

translated us into the kingdom of his dear Son: In
whom we have redemption through his blood, even
the forgiveness of sins: Who is the image of the
invisible God, the firstborn of every creature: For by
him were all things created, that are in heaven, and
that are in earth, visible and invisible, whether they
be thrones, or dominions, or principalities, or
powers; all things were created by him, and for him:
And he is before all things, and by him all things
consist. And he is the head of the body, the church:
who is the beginning, the firstborn from the dead;
that in all things he might have the preeminence. For
it pleased the Father that in him should all fulness
dwell; And, having made peace through the blood of
his cross, by him to reconcile all things unto himself;
by him, I say, whether they be things in earth or
things in heaven. (Col. 1:1-20)

In writing about praying for the saints, Paul uses the word
proseuchomai, which means to supplicate and make petition
before God. Then he uses the Greek word *aiteo*, which means
to ask for a particular thing to be given. Paul and Timothy were
asking that God would *work* in the saints, and that He would
give to the saints. The reason such prayers were necessary,
Paul pointed out, was that the saints had made their faith
known; they had appropriated Jesus for their lives.

The church today has the same responsibility toward the
ones who have sold out to Jesus. When young people who are
dedicated and filled with the Holy Spirit go out to the beaches
to hand out tracts and talk to kids about the Lord, the enemy is
going to launch a greater attack on their lives than he would if
they were just nominal Christians, warming a pew somewhere.
Because of the love of the sold-out ones for God's children, and
because of their love for Him, we have to pray that God will

protect them from all harm.

When I see a man or woman in whom I recognize a deposit of God—a knowledge of His truth and an ability to impart it to others—I begin to pray for that person, because I know the enemy is working too, to try to discourage him and pull him under.

I go into some churches where I'm not led to pray for them afterward because I can see there's no need to bother. The devil isn't challenged at all by the lukewarm faith evidenced there. In other churches, I find such a high level of praise and ministry to the Lord, that my spirit cries out, "Lord, keep that pastor straight. Be with every board member, every elder, every worker, every teacher, every leader, every usher, every hostess, every member of the choir. . . ." I pray for each one because I know that church is a threat to the enemy.

Paul was saying, "Listen, boys, we've heard about your walk with God. We've heard about your pulling apart from those who were steeping themselves in mere earthly knowledge. We've heard that you've separated yourselves from them and that you have tremendous love for one another. We've heard that Christ is evident in your lives, and for this cause, Timothy and I are praying for you now."

In this passage of Scripture, Paul is praying for the saints to have the knowledge of God's will in all wisdom and spiritual understanding (v. 9). He is talking about a knowledge superior to the usual kind of knowledge, a knowledge beyond the comprehension of man in the natural, a knowledge that exceeds anything he could read in a book or learn from listening to one of God's servants, a supernatural knowledge which is given by God to guide them continually. There are **too** many principalities and powers of darkness abroad in the world today for us to get by with the knowledge that used to be sufficient for us.

In asking that God will grant them wisdom, he's asking that

the mind of Christ will suffuse their minds with His own. Today we're hearing a lot about TM, which is Satan's counterfeit for what God wants for His people. Our prayer for the saint ought to be, "Lord, cause the whole mental faculty of my brother or sister to be so saturated with you that they can meditate on the purposes of God. Let them be quiet and have their minds pierced with your message, Lord."

We used to be able to have all the intellectual answers to man's questionings written out. We'd carry the lists of answers around in our Bibles. But today we don't do that because people are asking questions no one has thought to write down, questions like, "Listen, if God is God, then how come this, that, and the other?" You can search all day and not find the answer in the Four Spiritual Laws. That's why we need the supernatural knowledge and wisdom of God. When we have that, we can open our mouths, and such knowledge will pour forth as to confound the wisest intellectual.

Every time someone asks me a question, I pray, "Lord, grant me your wisdom." His wisdom is guaranteed to be available to us in abundant measure when we ask for it (James 1:5).

The spirit of counsel rested upon Jesus, the spirit of wisdom and understanding, of might and power and knowledge and of the fear of the Lord, according to Isaiah 11:2. These things are available to us also. We don't have to run along in our own lives limited by our own natural capacities. If God puts us in a position of ministry, He provides all we need to accomplish it.

I had a friend who wasn't aware of these things. She had served as the teacher of a ladies' Bible class for years, but never felt very anointed in her teaching. She thought she was dull, and everybody agreed with her. After she was filled with the Holy Spirit, I invited her to speak to a church group.

"Oh, I could never do that!" she protested.

"Let me give you a principle," I told her. "Whenever God

calls you to minister and He places you in a position of responsibility, He always equips you for the job to which He has called you." When she came in to speak, we put her in the prayer chair, laid hands on her, and reminded her that the power of God was going to be ministering through her.

It happened, just like that. She made the Word live as she spoke it forth that day. (And nobody thought she was dull.)

We are also to pray that the saints will have spiritual understanding (*sunesis*=insight), that they will know right from wrong. That kind of discernment has never been more important than it is today. False teaching can be so subtle that even the very elect can be deceived by it. We need to have understanding so we can sort things out. Suppose a great man of God stands before you and says something that doesn't line up with what you know to be God's Word. Should you receive his teaching just because you believe the man is basically sound? No, this is exactly why we need discernment, so as not to be led astray by personalities. The Holy Spirit doesn't want us to live in fear that we'll be seduced by wrong doctrines, wringing our hands and wailing, "I don't know *who* to trust any more." He wants us to use our God-given discernment, and check everything with the Word of God and with the witness of the Spirit within us. That way, we don't have to rely on the teacher's integrity or the reputation of a certain periodical or publishing house. We can judge for ourselves—this part is right, and this part is wrong—and thank God we know which is which.

Paul prayed the Colossians would know God's will in order that they might walk worthy of the Lord. Walk (*peripateo*) means to order our behavior properly. We all have to learn to do that.

In the Song of Solomon, the maiden who represents the church is seeking for her beloved. She encounters a group of daughters of Jerusalem—persons in the church, but not deeply involved with the Lord of the church—who ask her, "What's going on? What are you so upset about? Why are you running back and forth and up and down?"

"I've got to find my beloved," she tells them.

They don't seem to get the point.

"What is thy beloved more than any other?" they ask her. "What's so great about Him?"

The questioners are like believers who have no concept of what it means to be in love with Jesus. They know Him as Savior. They may even know that He loves them, but they don't know that they love Him.

The maiden tries to answer her questioners on an intellectual level, describing His attributes, but they can't understand her because those who are not lovers cannot understand the language of love. In the same way, much of the church today does not have any understanding of what it means to be in love with Jesus. That's why they find it so easy to walk without trying to be pleasing to Him, to do things that hurt Him. Paul was praying that such would not be the case in the lives of the saints, but that their devotion to Him, their love for Him, might show in how they walked before Him.

As we pray that the successful saints might walk worthy of the Lord, we're saying, "Come up higher. Get that imperfect thing out of your life. Come into the fulness and completion Jesus has for you. Get rid of what you are doing that is not pleasing to God. That is not where you want to walk. If you want to minister light every time you speak, if you want the power of the Holy Spirit in your life and the anointing of God on you, walk worthy of Him."

Jesus told a story about some men who had been given certain talents. One hid his talent in the sand. He was, in effect, saying, "Pray for me that I'll hold on to the end, brother. Pray that I'll be able to keep all that God placed in my care."

I'll never pray that for anybody. Instead, I'll pray, "Lord, let everything you have given this man flow out of him to bless your people." I know that the more he gives out, the more he'll receive from God.

Knowing the will of God is not difficult, but walking in it may be the hardest thing we've ever attempted. We can find out the will of God in a matter of moments sometimes.

"Thank you, Jesus, for giving me a knowledge of your will," we might say, satisfied we know which way to go. But instead of going there, we stall, asking, "Please, Lord, would you mind confirming it out of the mouth of two or more witnesses?"

That's no trouble for Him, and so He does it. But we're still not satisfied. We're still not ready to be obedient. What harm our disobedience does to the body of Christ!

As I travel about the United States, I often hear stories that begin like this:

"Well, I used to believe all that business about Jesus making people into new creatures and about the Holy Spirit coming to change us from one degree of glory to another, but we had a pastor in our church who—" They go on to tell about some misappropriation of funds, some immoral conduct, or something else less than the standards to which God is calling us. Over and over again I hear how bad conduct on the part of one of God's servants has been the enemy's means of drawing many away from the faith to which God had called them. How the work of God is hindered when we don't walk worthy of our calling!

We need to pray continually for one another that we will be able to discipline our lives to the point where we will live right, do right, think right, feel right, look right, and be right in the sight of the believers and the world. I need to see your chaste way of life; you need to see me live before you in line with the things that come out of my mouth when I am in the pulpit. Seeing right living in another person produces faith in us: "If she can live it, I can live it. If he can live it, I can too."

God uses His people to build one another up, to encourage one another. We literally provoke one another to love and good works (Heb. 10:24). "Provoke" means to agitate or stir up, and God says we are to do just that. We should be so good that other people will be ashamed not to measure up to the standard they see in our lives.

We need to pray, "Lord, teach your servants to shun the very appearance of evil. Teach them to walk uprightly before you. And don't let their right living lead them into the sin of pride."

Next, we need to pray that the saints will have pure hearts, that the fruit of love, joy, peace, cheerfulness, longsuffering, kindness, meekness, temperance and faith will be manifested in their lives. These are all by-products of the presence of the Lord. Christ in us, by His Spirit, produces these attributes that are foreign to the natural man in his carnal nature but not foreign to the God who created him.

Most of us would rather inspect the fruit than pray for the fruit to be manifested in the lives of others. We go around checking up on people, muttering, "I detect insincerity in him. I can tell there's no real flow of love in her." But Paul knew if two would agree, touching in the name of Jesus, they could have what they asked for. That means if we will really pray that the fruit of the Spirit be shown in the lives of our fellow Christians, it will come to pass.

When we begin to pray that kind of prayer for each other, criticism will go out the window. If we will begin to pray for somebody we're likely to criticize, we'll see a change in their lives, and in our own.

Next, Paul says he was praying for the saints to increase in the knowledge of God (v. 10). The bigger our God, the more we are able to ask of Him. Our God doesn't change, of course, but our concepts of Him do. When I go to pray and say, "O Lord," sometimes He reminds me of some area in my life where I'm still holding out, some area where I have not let Him *be* Lord.

"You're still hanging on to that, Iverna," He might say. And when I give up that area, and then another, I'm in line to ask for more blessings, and I'm in a position to receive them. Gradually, I'm learning to believe in a great omnipotent God who can do exceeding abundantly, above all I can ever ask Him.

To pray that the saints might not stagnate but grow, we might pray, "O God, let this minister, let this lay person, have an increased concept of who you are. Let them see you magnified beyond anything they have understood about you before. Let the prejudices crumble that have built walls and created stagnant pools. Let the way of the Lord be made full and clear and sweet."

We are also to pray that the saints might be strengthened with all might, according to His glorious power, unto all patience and longsuffering with joyfulness (v. 11). In praying that, we're asking that they might be empowered with the might of God.

Strength is the inherent power a person has to do a job, the outward display of ability. "His glorious power" is *kratos*, a power which is manifested openly.

When we have been "strengthened with all might, according to his glorious power," two things will be produced in us—patience in respect to things, and longsuffering, which is patience toward people. One commentator has described longsuffering as "a long holding out of the mind before it moves in action or passion." That takes God's power, all right, in some of the situations that confront us.

Take the case of a well-to-do jeweler. He never dressed like a successful merchant; his clothes were actually tacky. One day when he was in Los Angeles, his car broke down. While it was being repaired, he walked along the streets window-shopping.

God and I

Finding himself in front of an automobile showroom, he stopped to look through the window at a sleek new Lincoln Continental with all the extras. A salesman came running out, ready with his sales spiel, but he stopped short when he noticed the man's attire.

"Oh, brother!" he said to himself as he beat a hasty retreat into the air-conditioned interior of the showroom. "That guy couldn't afford a motorcycle, let alone a Continental. Why should I waste my breath on him?"

But the jeweler kept on looking at the car, then walked into the showroom for a closer inspection. He opened the door of the automobile, felt the upholstery, read all the information on the window sticker, even checked under the hood while the salesmen huddled in a corner, swapping jokes, wondering when the man would get his disreputable self out of their gleaming showroom.

In the meantime, a young salesman, new on the force, walked back into the building after his lunch hour.

"May I help you, sir?" he asked the jeweler, paying no attention to his seedy appearance. The jeweler asked him a lot of knowledgeable questions about the gas guzzler, got polite and knowledgeable answers from the young man, and promptly wrote out a check for the full purchase price of the car. The other salesmen almost passed out with shock.

The jeweler hadn't been threatened by their treatment of him because he knew who he was. He had power—the authority to be there—and in his bank account he had the ability to purchase anything he wanted. Apparently, he had developed the trait of longsuffering, too, somewhere along the line. Chances are, the salesmen learned something about not judging men by their outward appearance that day.

God wants His church to have the patience and longsuffering that come from knowing who we are in Him. He wants us to go through life knowing that whatever happens, the God within us

172

is more than adequate to get the job done. We can walk confidently and fearlessly into any situation if we're walking uprightly in Him.

Our patience and longsuffering are to be accompanied with joyfulness (v. 11), Paul says. Joy is considered the mark of Christian maturity. The word for joy in this passage is *chara*, and it means a calm cheerfulness in the face of whatever circumstances come our way. It's a result of knowing whom we have believed, and being persuaded that He is able to keep this life that we have committed unto Him (2 Tim. 1:12).

Will there come untoward circumstances? Guaranteed. But we'll have the patience to handle them with joy. Will there come pressures from people? Of course. But the longsuffering that is the fruit of the Spirit will enable us to withstand "people pressures" without blowing our tops, because we *know* that He is working all things together for our good (Rom. 8:28).

Finally, Paul says he prays that the saints might be filled with gratitude, "giving thanks unto the Father, which hath made us meet to be partakers of the inheritance of the saints in light" (v. 12).

God the Father, through Jesus Christ, the Son, has made us meet—ready, able, fit, and prepared—to be inheritors of everything the saints have been promised. And we are to give thanks to Him, and pray that our fellow-believers might give thanks as well, because a thank-filled life prevents a pride-filled life. Pride leads to destruction, and a lack of humility causes many a downfall.

Some years ago, I had barely managed to survive a baseless rumor about me, one I couldn't disprove. I'd felt whipped and beaten and defeated because of the lie that was spread. In the church one night, a minister from a foreign country walked up to me and said, "Iverna, I have a word from God for you."

I listened eagerly because I respected his walk with the Lord, and I certainly needed a word of encouragement. But that was hardly what he handed me.

"God wants to deal with your high-mindedness and pride," he told me.

"My high-mindedness and pride?" I sputtered, thinking I must have heard wrong. "Why, I hardly have enough oomph to survive. There's not an ounce of pride left in me."

I called to my brother Jud and asked him to come to hear the man's "word from the Lord."

"Go ahead, tell my brother what you told me," I said to the visiting minister. He repeated his message, and Jud just stood there shaking his head.

"I trust your walk with God," Judson told him, "but I think you've got your wires crossed this time. I know my sister well, and if I see anything in her life right now, it isn't pride. This gal has. . . ." He went on to say all kinds of good things about me to build me up. I stood there, drinking it in, thinking, "Jud's right. All those good things about me are true. You see there? I'm not proud at all."

When I went home that night, it was with a perfectly clear conscience, with a sense of having been completely vindicated. But I did pray about it, rather sanctimoniously, I'm afraid. "Lord, if that was you, I pray you'll reveal it to me." I just knew God would give me a clean bill of health just as Judson had.

But, oh! During the next few days, I saw such awful pride in me that I couldn't believe it. God was revealing it, all right, far more than I had any desire to see or to deal with. Furthermore, He showed me that my pride was rooted in the very situation I thought had wiped it out of me. I was proud of having been dragged through the knothole of false accusation. I was walking along with a high-minded attitude that I was a little better than the average run of people precisely *because* I had endured a trial.

Pride is such a subtle thing. Giving thanks to the Father, and praying for one another are two of the most helpful safeguards against it.

When we see pride in a fellow Christian, instead of praying, "Lord, deliver so-and-so from that foolish pride," we ought to pray, "God, cause so-and-so to be thankful to you. Open her eyes to see that everything she has, she has in you. Remind her that you lifted her up out of the miry clay and set her feet on the solid rock who is Jesus. Bring to her remembrance that without any merit on her part, you poured every bit of your grace and mercy into her life. O God, make her thankful daily."

As we pray, with Paul, that God will get the church in divine order with himself, and rightly related to one another, we won't have to worry about sinners being born again into newness of life. God already knows the names of the ones He's going to call. He has them all written down. And when the church has come into such a high degree of maturity that it can wisely parent newborn babes in Christ, there's going to be an influx of baby Christians above our fondest dreams.

When we think about the need for salvation of lost souls, we need to keep praying, "Lord, work in me to show them Jesus Christ." And just as He promised, He will give us the heathen for our inheritance.

Make prayer a part of your life, and I will pour out a blessing upon you and do mighty works and wonders such as you have never seen. My ways are higher than your ways. My thoughts are higher than your thoughts. Trust me, try me, believe me, and see what I will do.

I am longing and waiting for you to turn to me with all your hearts.

Believe, and make my power real in your lives. Let the well I have planted within you spring forth, pouring rivers of living water out of your inmost being. Let the power of the Holy Spirit come forth from your life to minister my life to my people.